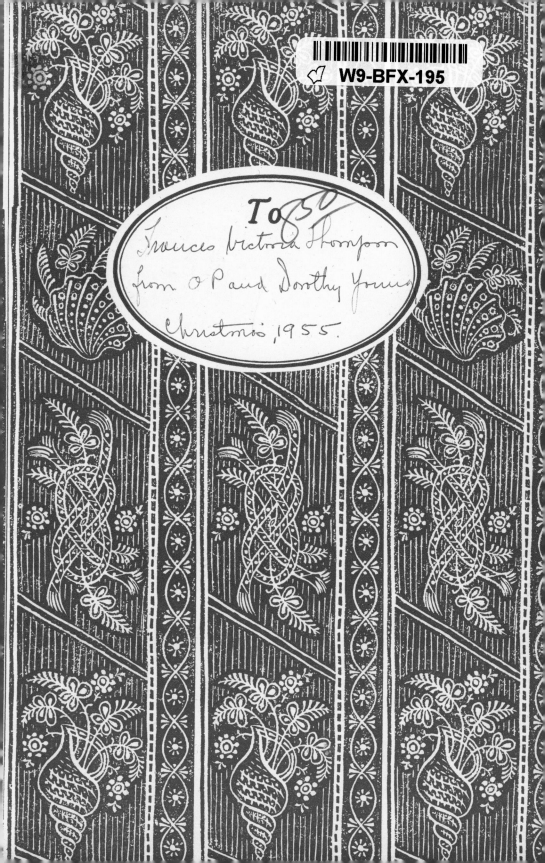

To

Frances Victoria Thompson
from O Paul Dorothy Young

Christmas, 1955.

THE SATURDAY BOOK

FIFTEENTH YEAR

THE
SATURDAY
BOOK

EDITED BY JOHN HADFIELD

15

Published by

THE MACMILLAN COMPANY

THIS FIFTEENTH ANNUAL ISSUE OF
THE SATURDAY BOOK is made and
printed in Great Britain at the
Mayflower Press (late of Plymouth),
at Watford, by William Brendon &
Son, Ltd. The type has been set at
the Gainsborough Press, St Albans,
by Fisher, Knight & Company, Ltd.
The four-colour plates were engraved
and printed by the Grout Engraving
Company, Ltd., at Bromley. The
book was bound by Greycaines
(Taylor, Garnett, Evans & Company,
Ltd.), at Watford.

PUBLISHED IN 1955

THE FRONTISPIECE reproduces Thomas
Gainsborough's portrait of Mary,
Countess Howe, at Kenwood, by
permission of the London County
Council, trustee of the Iveagh Bequest.

INTRODUCTION

AST YEAR a journal which always takes an acid view of established institutions remarked that 'the fourteenth *Saturday Book* gives out its usual aroma of *Vogue* smartness and values.' Although the reviewer's prose style made us wince a little we were not so nettled by this comparison as we imagine he intended us to be. Indeed, we were rather flattered by it.

Our editorial duties throw us much into the company of enthusiasts, specialists, collectors, and students of the curious. Charming people though they are, the last thing one would say of most of them is that they are 'smart.' As they gallop their hobby-horses through our pages we sometimes glance enviously at the self-possessed horsewomen, with Tautz-tailored habits and film-star seats, who trot like dream figures by Constantin Guys or Chalon through the glittering pages of *Vogue*.

We admit to an ungrudging admiration for *Vogue*. We have no prejudice at all against *the* vogue (without the capital letter). And we are only too conscious of our failures to come to terms with it. How galling it was, for instance, that our social and pictorial survey of the 'Twenties (in number 12) appeared two whole years before *The Boy Friend* put the 'Twenties on the map. And when *Genevieve* came along, to prove the most popular film comedy of our time, we had already gone to town on vintage cars and locked them away in number 13.

We wish we could be as smart as our acidulous critic says we are. We'd love to make a firm date with Fashion. In so doing we shouldn't feel in the least disloyal to her cousin Taste, with whom we like to think we have a permanent understanding. Indeed—who knows ?— they might even prove to be one and the same person. Unless we are much mistaken this is precisely what did happen when Gainsborough painted our frontispiece. Even *Vogue* has never printed anything smarter than this. J. H.

PS. Since the last *Saturday Book* came out we have persuaded Edwin Smith and Olive Cook to gather together into one book the cream of their contributions during the past ten years. It is now published : an assembly of some 250 pictures, with the title *Collectors' Items from The Saturday Book*. As an indulgent reviewer said of our own last number, 'just holding it makes one feel a thousand-a-year better off'.

THE CONTENTS

THE SATURDAY BOOK STORIES

SPECIMENS OF ART AND NATURE

THE CABINET OF INVENTIONS

A PICTURESQUE TOUR OF MERRIE ENGLAND

The decorations are by
FAITH JAQUES

[7]

THE SATURDAY BOOK'S POEM
WITH WOOD ENGRAVINGS
BY JOAN HASSALL

A SEDATIVE AT DAYBREAK

by LAURENCE WHISTLER

HERE, AGAIN !—One splintered second
By the wakening mind is reckoned
Ample to assume it all :
Shadowy table, ceiling, wall,
England, Europe, Infinite Space,
Human History, Hell, and Grace.
Proof of Mind's dominion, yes,—
And remembrancer, no less,
Of its bondage. For the beauty
Is, one must report for duty
Whether 'minded' to, or no ;
And, with five dull wits to show,
Answer for survival. So—
Adsum ! Ici ! Pronto ! Sto !
Present and correct !
                                But oh,

What a hubbub whistles in
Through that window ! What a din
Electrifies the darkness ! What
Rumour has the garden got—
Very Late Night Special—hot
News of something that was not
Dreamed, nor will be soon forgot :
Something glorious beyond all
Reckoning ? What do they bawl
In the branches—Death's Recall ?
Sudden Breach in Eden's Wall ?
Cancellation of the Fall ?

The panes reluctantly allow
Some vision's in the garden now.
The window, tentatively square,
Suggests that dawn is only there
By innuendo of blind air ;
Or as a concept in the mind
Of tired darkness, undefined ;
Or as the deep, vibrating chord
That Chaos knew, before the Word.

Yet that dark air is thickly scored
For brilliant jubilation : scratched,
Scribbled over, stippled, hatched,
Asteriskily affrighted,
Flourished, starred and twi-high-lighted,
By noise : by news : by nouns and notes
That spark and bubble in dark throats.
From orchard, meadow, marsh and clearing,
Flushed and dove-tailed into hearing,

Flashing, fading, reappearing—
Name them all you can't—though look who
Simplifies the task : a cuckoo
Out on orbit may be heard,
Threading dusk with one gold word,
Round as planets . . . Now, a wren
Lit by the sill . . . This blackbird, then,
Still haunted by his April theme . . .
And there the thrush, whose phrases seem
To flicker with his own sunbeam.

The thrush, enlightener of the dark,
The blackbird illustrating Bach,
The wren exploding into praise,
The chaffinch blissful with one phrase,
The curlew bubbling from a cloud,
The robin thinking thoughts out-loud,
The swift amazed at his own speed,
The starling glorified in greed,
The storm-cock pinnacled for shouting,
The tawny owl at dawn of doubting,
The thrush illumining the world,
The robin noting buds are pearled,
The blackcap's nimble sweet contralto,
The blackbird's almost human alto,
The green woodpecker's jubilee laugh,
The jay's reply in withering chaff,
The sparrow's cheep, engaging toy,
The cuckoo's perfect word for joy,
The willow-warbler's plaintive scale,
The heart-ache of the nightingale,
The cuckoo's pass-word to far summer,
The snipe's tattoo, the distant drummer,
The yellow-hammer's roadside greeting,
The nightingale's divine entreating,
The magpie's ill-appointed clatter,
The blackbird with a tune to scatter,
The thrush irradiating day,
The robin commenting on May,

The skylarks fingering heaven's edge,
The yellow-hammer's wistful hedge,
The corny bunting's pizzicato,
The day-and-nightingale's legato,
The whitethroat's tune in fiddle-snatches,
The blackbird's roundelazy catches,
The dunnock's commongrace of ditty,
The starlings' ways-and-means committee.
The skylarks fingering silver combs,
The martins muttering in their homes,
The swallows murmuring mild and high,
The -catcher whispering to the fly,
The ring-dove, rhythmic in the trance,
The robin's brief, observant glance,
The turtle-dove's patrician dolour,
The starling's loud defence of squalor,
The rook's dry comment and the crow's,
The one urbane, the one morose,
The wren, in gusto absolute,
The goldcrest shriller, but minute,
The playful pe- of scattered -wits,
The total tattle of tom-tits,
The gossiping of farmyard fowls,
The heavy breathing of young owls,
The rooster's swank, the gander's honk,
The blackbird's hint of César Franck,
The kingfisher with one bright cry,
The thrush like all a brightening sky,
The nuthatch, flicking stones on ice,
The robin tempering sound advice,
The blackcap's virtuoso flute,
The oh-so-cacophonic coot,
The bunting's tinkle from a reed,
The moorhen's clangour and stampede,
The warblers by the water's ledge,
The reed- more tranquil than the sedge-,
The marsh- with finer tone and skill,
The grasshopper- more whiz than trill,
The greenfinch with a bagpipe squeeze,

The starling with his bronchial wheeze,
The blackbird with a score to quote,
The thrush with sunrise in his throat,
The rooks around the tent of dawning,
The swifts that smooth the enormous awning,
The larks that lift its rippling crown,
The cocks that peg the skylines down,

The goldfinch, beaded water-spout,
The wren like runnels after drought,
The great tit whetting his bright saw,
The linnet like a larch in thaw,
The wood-lark fluting, soft and ripe,
The garden-warbler's bubble-pipe,
The chiffchaff pleased with his own name,
The thrush, with easting heart aflame,
The blue tit's double-pipe and skirr,
The green hilarious woodpecker,
The corn-crake somnolently grating,
The spotted woodpecker vibrating,
The five horizons of the cocks,
The cuckoo's vows (unorthodox),
The meadow-pipit's fading trill,
The blackbird diatonic still—
And still the thrush, no spark abating,
But light itself illuminating :
The mottled cry, the vocal gleam,
The minim ray, the quavered beam ;
Light orchestration of the small,
Illuminumerable all . . .

Yes, the pillow. Yes, more in—
But down and in—and next the chin.

Yes, the sheet a trifle slacker :
Close the port-holes on the fracas.
Yes, or very nearly yes :
Still some matter for distress :
Falling short of full success :
Lack of absolute finesse :
Eiderdown in some excess ?
Well, no matter, more or less :
Too unspecified to guess :
Too generic to express :
Too habitual to assess :
Too remote, now, to redress :
(Too much bliss for true distress).
Better, far, to acquiesce,
Act of grace, to acquiesce,
Verb synonymous with bless,
Verb of quasi-saintliness,
Vocables of pure caress :
Acqui ripe as velvet esce,
Acqui sleek as silken dress,
Acqui crisp as watercress,
Aquatinted aquacress . . .
Aquatint or Aquitaine ?
Aqueduct and aquaplane,
Equatorial equitation,
Equiangular equation,
Oxymoron oxyless,
Wake me at tu quoque, yes.

Yes, indeed. And as you slide
Into Sleep's odd countryside,
While a-carefree-gain you sink
Over Eider's downland brink,
While your notions, crossed with follies,
Romp and streak away like collies,
While your happy heart-beats tramp
Down from daybreak's British Camp,
And with measured foot-fall sally
Into Snore's primeval valley—
Clock may crow and bird may chime,
Sun may hoot and factory climb,
Tractor yodel, milkman drum,
Steeple yap and spaniel hum,
Boy rev up and Bentley shout . . .
They've heard your *fiat* : 'Count me out !'
Your wish is on the whitening sill :
'Don't disturb me !' Nothing will.

Little could, in your condition :
Short, that is, of nuclear fission.
Not in all these hours of sleep
Have you rambled down so deep
Where the ferns of fiction blind
Ancient landslips of the mind.
There, should some remote unease
Touch you, like a spectral breeze,
Whispering—'Beside your bed
Something waits your lifted head :
Something welcome, something wet,
Something hot'—allay the fret !
Turn the doubt on which it plays
Into flowering paraphrase,
And by figurative ways
Deeper into dreams recoil . . .
Your early cup will never spoil.
Though yet unsipped, it takes no chill ;
Though madly tipped, it cannot spill—
It hangs upon the dresser still !

And all's inertia that will be
Coactive for that cup of tea.
The saucer's deep among the crocks ;
The match undisparate in the box ;
The kettle haunts the fairy ring,
But, short of fairies, waits to sing.
As for the rest, you may suppose
These quite as uninvolved as those.
The gas, it may be, hardly stirs
In dawn's maroon gasometers ;
The milk, perhaps, is in the cow ;
The tea—who knows ?—in junk or dhow ;
The sugar's scarcely out of cane ;
And even the water—even the plain
White water's in the whispering main !

Not soon the crisis, then. Not soon
Rewarded loss, and dubious boon.
Not soon will come ambivalent up,
Unwanted, welcome, wide, the cup.
Yet come it will.—And, peradventure,
It won't incur one glance of censure,
While rounding off the script of dream
With certain flourishes of steam.

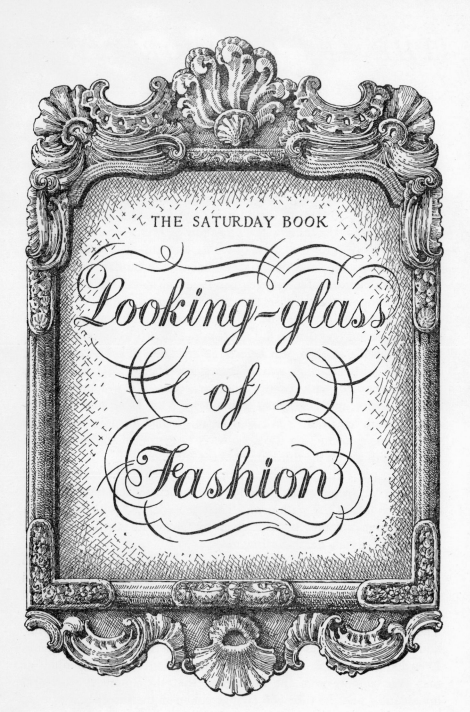

THE SATURDAY BOOK

Looking-glass
of
Fashion

THE ART OF ADORNMENT

by EDWIN SMITH & OLIVE COOK

Chains, coronets, pendants, bracelets and ear-rings,
Pins, girdles, spangles, embroideries and rings.

HESE, according to a pastoral performed at Norwich in 1631, were the customary adornments of a beauty of the period. The requirements of a lady of today or two thousand years ago might be listed in exactly the same way. And, now as ever, the same curiously mixed motives of vanity and humility, sentiment and superstition prompt the desire to embellish the human body. The goldsmith's methods of setting gems and working metals have undergone as little change as the purposes for which jewellery is made. Variation is only to be found in style and in preferences at different periods. A sixteenth-century gentleman did not consider his attire complete without ear-rings, while in 1880, just before the invention of the screw device, a woman with ear-rings was overdressed. Henry VIII sat for his portrait adorned with twenty gold bracelets. The hands of the English ladies and gentlemen painted by Van Dyck and Lely are conspicuously ringless. *The Young Ladies' Journal* for 1869 informs us that an engagement ring should always be worn on the second and not, as we think, on the third finger of the left hand.

No personal relics are more stirring than jewels. The undiminished splendour with which they shine long after their owners have returned to dust enhances the pathos and passion associated with such relics as the sardonyx cameo portrait given by Queen Elizabeth I to Essex, or Caesar Borgia's death-dealing ring.

Jewels are instinct with a life of their own, life drawn from the hidden recesses of the earth where millions of years before man emerged glittering gems and precious metals were created by the clash of mighty chemical forces. Undoubtedly some stones are hostile to mankind. The Hope Diamond brought disaster to all who possessed it. Strange and special properties have always been ascribed to certain gems. Even today a woman may well hesitate to don the baleful opal, or may take comfort from the knowledge that the amethyst wards off intoxication, and the ruby will change colour in the presence of poison.

[18]

Opposite : Three antique cameos and jewellery of the 18th, 19th, and 20th centuries, from Cameo Corner

With the exception of the early Greek bronze armlet these examples of Greek and Etruscan jewellery are fashioned entirely of gold. The Etruscan seventh-century B.C. votive bracelet (*left*) and the Greek ear-ring (*foot of page*) of *c*. 420 B.C. show the extraordinary skill, mystifying to modern craftsmen, attained by

the Aegean peoples in granulated ornament, while the head of a river god from a late Etruscan necklace (*above*) illustrates their command of embossed work. The fine Greek ring of the fifth century B.C. (*within the armlet*) is a rarity ; rings were worn sparingly at that period and were restricted to the third finger of the left hand. (*British Museum.*)

a

b

c

(*a*) Greek gold ear-ring with figure of Eros, (*b*) Etruscan gold plaque from a necklace showing Dionysos, (*c*) Gold diadem from Rhodes, late 7th cent. B.C., (*d*) Plaque from an Etruscan necklace or girdle, (*e*) Etruscan gold necklace, 6th–7th cent. B.C. (B.M.) and (*f*) Greek gold pendant with head of Medusa (Louis Meier).

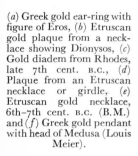

d

f

e

Shell ritual ornaments from the Belgian Congo, and (below) English 19th-cent. bead-work (Louis Meier).

African collars of cowrie shells and bead-work, two bead-work necklaces and an apron (Fred Uhlman and Josef Herman)

(a) Visigothic (?) gilt bronze buckle set with garnets, 6th cent.
(V. & A.), (b) Gold badge from Ashanti, 19th cent., (c) New
Zealand greenstone tiki, (d) Mexican stone pendant (all B.M.),
(e) Frankish brooch set with garnets, 6th cent. (V. & A.), (f)
Gold ornament from Ashanti (V. & A.) and (g) Shell ear-ring
from Borneo (B.M.). Below, turtle-shell discs from New Guinea.

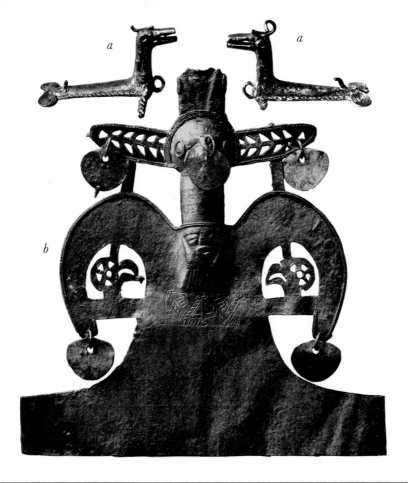

(*a*) Columbian gold ear-rings, (*b*) Columbian gold ornament, (*c*) Mixtec pendant (all B.M.), (*d*) Anglo-Saxon gold and silver filigree brooch with garnet and lapis inlay (V. & A.), and (*e*) and (*f*) gold ornaments from Ashanti, 19th cent.

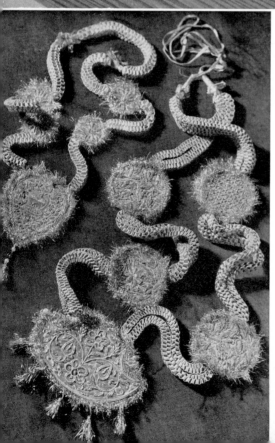

Syrian silver ear-rings, 20th cent. (Sarah Nechamkin), and a gold bracelet, such as the lady opposite wears, with Syrian scenes made in Victorian London by John Brogden (V. & A.). Opposite, below: 19th-cent. Indian brooch, and an Egyptian pectoral ornament with a French 18th-cent. setting (Louis Meier).

The King's
Daughter :
coloured
lantern
slide
(*Coll. Roger
Musgrave*)

Jewish, 16th cent.

Jewish 17th cent.

Roman 3rd cent.

English 18th cent.

Anglo-Saxon 9th cent.

English
early 19th
cent.

Roman 4th cent.

English 18th cent.

Etruscan
3rd cent.
B.C.

Victorian necklace of Whitby jet, Egyptian scarab ring with French gold mount (*Louis Meier*), English eighteenth-century gold ring set with a garnet and an English eighteenth-century marriage ring.

Two Etruscan gold wreaths, (a) from the third century B.C. and (c) from the fifth century B.C. ; (b) a coronet of tortoiseshell and ivory from the islands of the Marquesas; (e) a Roman sardonyx cameo of Augustus whose fillet of gold and gems was added during the Middle Ages (all from the British Museum); (d) a headdress of diamonds and feathers advertised by the Parisian Diamond Company in 1898.

Italian, French, Spanish and English Renaissance jewellery (Victoria and Albert Museum)

Detail from *Lucretia* by Lotto, *c.* 1530 (National Gallery)

Venus by Cranach, 1530 (Vienna Mus.), the Heneage Armada Jewel, enamelled gold with miniature of Queen Elizabeth, by Hilliard, *c.* 1588 (V. & A.) and the Tor Abbey Jewel, enamelled gold, inscribed 'Through the Resurrection of Christe we be all sanctified,' 1560 (V. & A.).

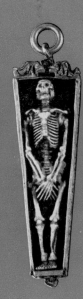

a

b

(*a*) Ellis Gamble's trade card engraved by Hogarth, (*b*) and (*c*) Sicilian silver gilt clasp and belt from Piano de' Greci, 18th cent., (*d*) English coral and gold necklace, late 18th cent. and Sicilian 20th-cent. coral and silver ring, (*e–h*) Italian onyx cameos, 18th cent. (V. & A.) and (*i*) French gold, enamel, pearl and diamond pendant, 18th cent. (Louis Meier).

The inspiration behind all these objects is classical; even the monumental Sicilian Madonna stands between Doric columns. The cameos not only represent classical subjects but are almost indistinguishable from antique cameos. The head of Ceres with a lighted torch and a bird signifying vigilance on the necklace may have been chosen to accord with the ancient tradition that coral brought prosperity and averted danger.

d

c

e

f

i

g

h

Italian butterfly necklace of marble mosaic plaques mounted in gold, *c.* 1820, an English gold, pearl and diamond pendant, *c.* 1830 (V. & A.), a 19th-cent. ear-ring of Whitby jet and an early Victorian necklace of silver and amethysts. Opposite, a brooch, ear-ring and buckle of Berlin ironwork and two mid-19th-cent. brooches and an ear-ring of iron wire-work (W. Ewer). Berlin ironwork dates from the time of the Napoleonic wars when the Prussian government presented such delicate iron ornaments to the people in return for jewels or gold.

In the portrait by Ingres, Madame Moitessier wears a gold and garnet brooch which is characteristic of the opulence of 19th-century jewellery. Among the Victorian onyx, cameo, coral and pearl ornaments opposite is a bracelet of pinchbeck, the alloy made by Christopher Pinchbeck in the early 18th cent,. and a necklace of cut steel made by Matthew Boulton of Birmingham at the close of the century (Frances Harling).

SCARF PINS.

Brilliants, £6.   Brilliants, £5.   Enamel on Gold with Diamond Eyes, £2. 10s.

Necklace and ear-rings of chrysoberyl and pinchbeck (Mrs Rutland)

A Choice Spirit

A Jessamy

A Blood

An Honest Fellow

From *The Follies of Man,* 1790

THE NATURAL HISTORY OF
THE SPIV

by C. WILLETT CUNNINGTON

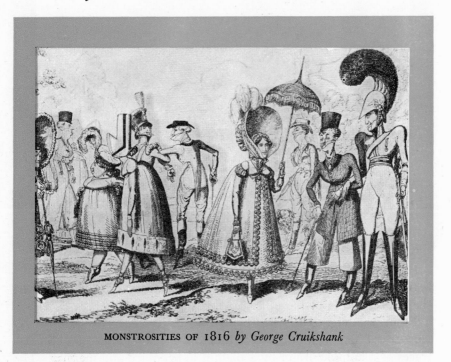

MONSTROSITIES OF 1816 *by George Cruikshank*

F YOU LOOK in the dictionary you will learn that 'spiffy' means 'sprucely clad,' and has been in colloquial use for centuries. We even find Lady Mary Wortley Montague describing a rival's dress as 'awfully spiff.' It is only our slovenly mode of speech that has debased spiff into Spiv.

Further research reveals that the social personality on whom we have conferred this time-honoured if now degenerate epithet used to own a distinctive surname which indicated his position in the social scale. He was called a 'fellow.' This implied that he was 'not quite.' To be addressed as a 'fellow' was an insult. In that heated battle of words

MUSICAL DANDIES 1835 *by George Cruikshank*

between Mr Pickwick and Mr Tupman each, you remember, hurled the offensive title at the other, apologizing afterwards.

From the eighteenth century onwards there have been many varieties of 'fellow,' but all have shared a common aim—to obliterate traces of a humble origin by a blatant appearance and manner. The ambition of all of them was to be distinguished from the Common Man. This laudable ambition persists today, and it is high time that the modern exponent ceased to be known merely by a corrupt adjective. He deserves a grammatical title which recognizes his ancestry and is both descriptive and melodious. These requirements, I suggest, would be met by the word 'Spiffellow.'

Like other leaders of Fashion your genuine Spiffellow has always had base imitators. Today there are the Teddy Boys, whose pseudo-Edwardian garb serves to remind us that a century ago, on smaller wages, they would have been content to sport slap-up benjies and kicksies cut saucy. But while the technique of the Teddy Boy is dynamic and is apt to depend on fists, knives or coshes, that of the true Spiffellow is static ; he is content simply to let his appearance hit you in the eye. In this there is the touch of the artist, expressing a symbolic protest against the democratic principle of Equality.

Perhaps it would comfort him to learn that his ancestors underwent a similar struggle, and received for their pains even more hostile criticism. Two centuries ago, in spite of the vast differences of wealth between the social groups, it was nevertheless possible to climb out of the crowd and get some way up the ladder. At each stage of the ascent the 'fellow' received a distinctive name.

Starting as a simple country bumpkin, with provincial accent, slouching gait, long lank hair and drab suit—called for short a Greenhorn—he could become, in urban surroundings, in turn a Jemmy, a Jessamy, a Dapper, a Smart, a Mettled Fellow, an Honest Fellow, a Joyous Spirit. If by luck or cunning enough wealth could be obtained, he might even rise to the glories of being a Buck or Blood.

For this arduous excursion a sound constitution and a good head for wine were essential, and many fell by the way or remained stuck on the lower rungs. At each step one had to learn fresh expletives. In the lower levels the novice employed such phrases as 'Rat it !', 'Fegs !' or 'Zookers !' These in turn would be discarded for the more elegant 'Zauns !', 'Ged's curse it !' and 'Demme !' With growing confidence the climber would soon change the latter to 'Damme !' ; which, we are told by a writer of the time, signified an appreciable advance.

With these stages in elocution went improvements in costume. Cut hair, a brown bob wig, coloured waistcoats, white thread stocking and a tailor-made suit sufficed the Jemmy. The Jessamy allowed the hair to grow long enough to be combed back over the foretop of the wig, which in the evening would be replaced by a queue with a black solitaire ribbon round the neck. A waistcoat edged with lace, silk stockings and clean gloves were adopted at this stage.

Dappers, we learn, wore coats of light broadcloth, calimanco or red waistcoats, a cane suspended from the fifth button, and 'a peculiar spring in their arms, a wriggle in their bodies, and a trip in their gait.' They had, in fact, a close resemblance to the Spiffellow of today, though he has not yet adopted red-heeled shoes. The Smart, one fears, is beyond modern emulation, for he wore a bag-wig and a sword ; if the latter was used frequently to pink a rival he became a Mettled Fellow. The Joyous Spirit had an aptitude for deep drinking, while the Honest Fellow was skilled in packing cards and cogging dice.

THE GENT, 1847

A very rare specimen, who seems to have flourished for only a few years about 1730, deserves to be recorded because his costume was in marked contrast to the stiff-fitting garments of the gentleman of *ton*, and in place of a sword he carried a cudgel. He was known as a 'Flap.' A letter from a footman in *The Auditor*, February 23, 1733, informs us that his master's 'eldest son is a most notorious Flap ; my master has converted me into one. I now wear a short wig to which my eyebrows are combed up, and pasted over it by way of Tupee. I wear my clothes so very genteel I have no shape but am all *Flap*, my waste beginning at my shoulders ; and my oaken stick is so long that I dont know what to do with it.'

Twenty years later we see a vast change, as described in *Pompey the Little* : 'His great ambition was to be deemed a jemmy fellow, for which purpose he appeared always in the morning in a Newmarket frock, decorated with a great number of green, red, or blue capes ; he wore a short bob wig, neat buck's-skin breeches, white silk stockings, and carried a cane switch.'

As we trace the species into the nineteenth century we discover among the exquisites of the Regency some capital specimens in Cossack trousers, Cumberland corsets, and 'winkers' up to the eyes, doing their best to resemble genuine Dandies. Sometimes, indeed, the most perfect examples of the breed were to be found among the aristocracy itself. For example, there was that early-Victorian marquis who appeared in the evening, 'his hair parted in the middle and falling in

[44]

ringlets about his ears, wearing a blue dress coat with velvet collar and cuffs and a bouquet in the buttonhole, a white cravat nestling among six point-lace frills of an embroidered shirt-front over a pink silk under-waistcoat, diamond studs chained together, an over-waist-coat of cerulean blue satin worked in hearts-ease and copiously hung with chains and seals, the buttons enormous blood-stones, pink silk stockings, and lace-trimmed handkerchief highly scented.' Although Victorian prudery prevented Surtees

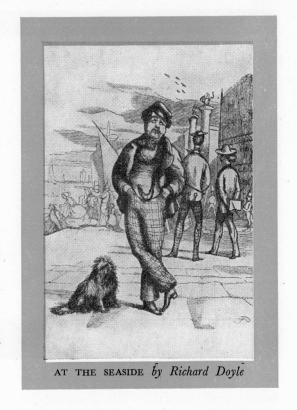

AT THE SEASIDE *by Richard Doyle*

from describing the nether integuments he does pronounce him to be 'a pretty Jemmy Jessamy sort of fellow,' and with this we are inclined to agree.

But the more general brands of 'Fellow' at that period were described by Albert Smith in his book, *The Natural History of the Gent*. 'Gent' had become the early-Victorian name for him, defined by that author as one who assumes 'a futile aping of superiority that inspires us with feelings of contempt and amusement.' He points out that the Gent is not to be confused with the Downey One or the Knowing Cove, who are his social inferiors. The Gent, we are told, had his peculiar figures of speech, and would address a pal with the phrase : ' 'Ullo, my P-ippin.' ' (Observe the subtle pause, equivalent to a crotchet rest, after the capital P. This required some practice to sound effective.) His costume had striking features ; he favoured, we are told, peg-top trousers in large checks, short coat and 'a staring shawl,' and carried a stick furnished with a silver horse's hoof on top. Thus attired he would

A DOWNY COVE AT TATTERSALLS, 1844, *by George Standfast*

fancy himself as 'all the Stilton,' ogling the girls, and puffing smoke in their faces.

Glance at his feet and observe the tight cloth boot, with patent leather toe, and a row of mother-of-pearl buttons down the front. Observe the marvellous cravat, a blue 'Joinville,' with rainbow ends controlled by gilt eels twisted round or gigantic pins. His studs are like blue raspberries. His finger-nails are none of the cleanest, but he wears yellow gloves on which are rings in profusion. He smokes a 'weed,' and is uncommonly noisy when he goes on a spree. On such occasions his shirt comes into the picture. One reads of the figure of an actress 'forming the pattern of his shirt on which she was reproduced many times in a chocolate tint.' At the seaside he may favour 'a shirt embroidered with pink boa-constrictors.'

The Spiffellow has always been closely associated with forms of sport, at which, however, he plays a spectator's part. The early-Victorian Gent could generally be found hovering about Tattersalls and similar horsey circles. There one could detect his variations by the garb worn.

[46]

'I'm a knowing card' was openly declared in the slang, turned-up hat shading his chubby cheeks and chubby nose, pleasantly adorned with stationary pimples. 'I'm a slap-up kiddy' was advertised in the blue and white spotted handkerchief twisted round his neck. 'I'm a downy cove' was portrayed in his Newmarket cutaway coat and long, very long, waistcoat. Even his straight legs, encased in tight-fitting cords, announced broadly 'we're inexpressibles of no ordinary stuff.'

A more exuberant specimen, in patent leather boots and glossy beaver hat, sported 'a colossal ruby pin in the strikingly attractive scarf emerging from the bosom like the inflated crop of a fancy pouter' and was addressed by his friends as 'Knowing Harry.' We accept the statement that he 'lived by his wits.'

The Gent, though not claiming to be the Heavy Swell of the period, had certainly succeeded in distinguishing himself from the Common Man. Unfortunately his distinction was not always advantageous. A magistrate at the time declared 'I hold a man who is called a "Gent" to be the greatest blackguard there is.'

By the end of last century the term Gent was becoming obsolete, and was replaced by Bounder, which was defined as 'a fellow you draw the line at.' Always these harsh words, you see.

Surely now in this drab world of ours, where the Spiffellow strikes such a cheerful note, with those resplendent shoulders and buttered hair, he deserves a more bonhommous welcome and a more savoury name than Spiv ! For my part, although I don't profess that he is exactly the apple of my eye, I intend in future to greet him with old-world courtesy and a hearty ''Ullo, my P-ippin !' Not omitting the capital P, and the crotchet rest.

Cartoon by Dana Gibson

THE RETURN OF THE BEARD

by MARY EDEN

'ORD, I could not endure a husband with a beard on his face : I had rather lie in the woollen.' Thus Beatrice in *Much Ado About Nothing*, and from a purely personal point of view I entirely agree with her. But beards are not a subject about which a mere woman can allow herself to indulge purely personal prejudices. Like the chins they adorn they are a natural phenomenon, as old as mankind. Despite the temptation to make frivolous observations, a woman must write of beards with a seemly detachment, or not at all.

When I first began to consider the place of beards in the history of fashion I was delighted to find that they were the subject of a special science. The pleasing name 'Pogonology,' by which this science is known, would appear to be an inspiration of that modern chronicler of beards, Reginald Reynolds, who has devoted a fascinating monograph to the subject. It is derived from *pogonias*, meaning bearded, a word common to both the Greek and Latin languages : and the fact that the Emperor Constantine was known as 'Pogonatus,' the bearded one, showed that many centuries ago the science was already well advanced.

Thus reassured of the respectable antiquity of our subject, let us consider a few highlights of its history. The first human beards were undoubtedly the undisciplined growths of the Old Stone Age. These, however, need not detain us here, for they were worn without sophistication, and existed in virgin profusion for the simple reason that men had not yet discovered the value of trimming them, training them, or otherwise improving on the work of nature. But as time went on pogonology evolved from this primitive condition. The beard became a symbol, an expression of personality and mood, which played an increasingly important role in social life.

In ancient times, when man had only just emerged from the twilight of prehistory, we find that the beard was already held in the highest esteem. It was a mark of wisdom, or a sign of strength, physical prowess and manly domination. Many eastern Mediterranean peoples swore

Abraham Lincoln and Disraeli exemplify contrasted styles of beard in favour among nineteenth-century statesmen on opposite sides of the Atlantic. The beards of Ernest Hemingway and Robert Gibbings suggest that, in the literary world at least, there has been a rapprochement.

There is a remarkable likeness between the beard worn by Sir Compton Mackenzie (above) and that shown in the seventeenth-century picture on the right by Van Dyck. Sir Compton Mackenzie's portrait was painted by R. H. Westwater, A.R.S.A., R.P., himself the wearer of a handsome beard. Little is known about Van Dyck's subject, Cornelius van der Geest, but his beard enhances the impression of dignity, gravity and courtly grace that are so characteristic of Van Dyck's work.

The long beard seems symbolic of a high-minded temperance. The picture of Charles Darwin on the left is by John Collier. El Greco's portrait on the right is of Luigi Cornaro, Venetian author of a treatise on longevity, who himself lived to be over a hundred. Shorter beards seem to be associated with more extrovert talents. Below are Alfred Drake, the American star of *Kismet* (whose beard is all his own), and Philip Harben, the Television chef.

THE BEARD ARTISTIC
Sir Thomas Beecham,
musician and wit

W. G. GRACE, 19th-century cricketer
DUNCAN CARSE, 20th-century explorer

THE BEARD MONARCHAL
King Charles the First
by Van Dyck

THE BEARD PROPHETIC
Ezekiel, from the ceiling
of the Sistine Chapel,
by Michelangelo

by their beards, and the kissing of beards was a sign of greeting, like the shaking of hands today. But to tweak a man's beard, or touch it in any other disrespectful way, was a deadly insult.

The Jews had particular reverence for the beard, and it was invariably worn by their sages and prophets. A fine growth of hair was regarded as a divine gift which it would be a sin to despoil. Only on very special occasions, and with the express permission of the Creator, could it be tampered with in any way. One such occasion was when God said to Ezekiel before he went to deal with the rebellious Israelites : 'Take thee a sharp knife, take thee a barber's rasor, and cause it to pass upon thine head and upon thy beard.'

In Greece and Rome it was the custom for a youth to dedicate his first growth of beard to the gods : and the beards of the Greek and Roman sages were as imposing as those of their Jewish counterparts. A man who could grow a beard as long as Socrates thought himself as great a philosopher. But evidently the real thinkers were not easily deceived by such pretensions. As Herodes Atticus dryly remarks in the second century A.D., 'I see the beard and the cloak, but I do not see the philosopher.'

There were a few exceptions in the ancient world to the otherwise universal cult of the beard. Thus the Egyptians, who loathed hair and looked on the wearing of it as a sign of uncleanliness, would not kiss the beard of a Greek. And Alexander the Great forbade his soldiers to wear beards to prevent their enemies getting hold of them and striking them down. Later, the prophet Mahommed ordered all his followers to shave off their beards to make clear their distinction from the Jews.

Throughout the history of pogonology the owners of beards have made them the subject of much loving care. For example, the early Persian kings used to plait their sacred beards with gold threads, while the trimming, curling and oiling of beards has been practised by dandies since the time of the Lords of Nineveh. In England, the peak of male vanity in beards was reached in the first part of the seventeenth century, when their care was the most important part of the daily toilet. Hours were spent in starching them, and curling them with quills and irons. Barbers cut men's beards according to the shapes of their faces, in the same way as the modern hairdresser cuts a woman's hair. Thus one contemporary pogonologist writes : 'If he be weasel-becked, then much hair left on the cheeks will make the owner look like a bowdled hen, and as grim as a goose. . . .'

Sometimes beards were exotically perfumed and even dyed in different colours. The favourite perfume was orris powder, which had a scent rather like violets, but subtler, and even more delicate. In order to protect the newly coiffured and scented beard at night the owner used to go to sleep with it securely enclosed in a leather case. Many-coloured beards were, of course, invaluable props in the Elizabethan theatre, as witness Bottom the Weaver accepting the part of Pyramus : 'I will discharge it in either your straw-colour beard, your orange-tawny beard, your purple-in-grain beard, or your French-crown-colour beard, your perfect yellow.'

With Cromwell and the Puritans beards began to go out of favour, and the powdered wigs and smooth chins of the eighteenth century took their place. It was not until the middle of Queen Victoria's reign that they began to return to popularity. This was an age of Great Men, and it is not surprising that with a new crop of sages there came a new crop of beards. The bushy Victorian beard also well symbolises the dominating, tyrannical husband of the kind to be found in Wimpole Street, and presumably elsewhere, whose wife crept about the house in fear, and whose children dreaded the anger that glowed perpetually in his hairy face.

But the beard in Victorian times was not only a symbol ; it had practical uses as well. For example, in 1853 a remarkable manifesto was issued by nine employees of the Scottish Central Railway. It was signed by two engine drivers, a fireman, an inspector of police, as well as no less than five guards, and read as follows :

'We, the servants of the Scottish Central Railway, beg to inform you, that having last summer seen a circular recommending the men employed upon railways to cultivate the growth of their Beards, as the best protection against the clemency of the weather, have been induced to follow this advice ; and the benefit we have derived from it, induces us to recommend it to the general adoption of our brothers in similar circumstances throughout the kingdom. We can assure them, from our own experience, that they will by this means be saved from the bad colds and sore throats of such frequent occurrence without this natural protection.'

The prosaic and utilitarian spirit in which these railwaymen approached the question of beards is enough to make the pogonological purist wince. But there are still worse examples of the degradation of the beard into a purely functional use. It has even been darkly hinted that W. G. Grace cultivated his famous growth with the express purpose of concealing the stumps from the eyes of Australia's fast bowlers—a suggestion which no true sportsman would credit for a moment. But there is little doubt that some men have been led to cultivate beards to hide weaknesses of feature or absence of chin.

From the feminine point of view, even for those women who are partial to beards, there are infinite dangers in marrying a man whose face has never been seen devoid of hair. There is, for instance, the sad story of the disillusionment of the wife of Jean Étienne Liotard, a Swiss painter of the time of George II, who one day unexpectedly shaved off his beard. His wife was completely horrified, for instead of the dignified and irresistibly handsome features she had known she saw a pinched little face, with a snub nose,

'And such a little perking chin
To kiss it seemed almost a sin !'

And now, to conclude, what of the position of the beard today ? At the end of the Victorian era it went once more into eclipse, lingering only on the chins of monarchs, artists, and a few unrepentant individualists. Now, however, it is showing signs of a revival. It can be seen in splendid variety on the faces of actors, chefs, explorers, musicians, and even participants in television panel games and contributors to the *Saturday Book*. Only among saints, scientists and sages does it seem to be neglected. The leaders in these fields remain for the most part firmly beardless, although whether this is due to a decrease in wisdom, or simply resentment at the wider distribution of beards among the rank and file, it would be rash to express an opinion. In any case, despite this failure by the few to keep abreast of the spirit of the times, there would seem to be little danger that the pogonologist of the future will suffer from lack of material for his researches. The star of Pogonatus, the bearded one, is once more in the ascendant.

The
Saturday
Book

PERSONAL

COLUMNS

EDDIE MARSH

THE COMPLETE EDWARDIAN

by LANCE SIEVEKING

T WAS in April, 1915, that I saw Eddie Marsh for the first time. Some months earlier, at the age of eighteen, I had joined the Artists' Rifles as a private, for no better reason than that every young man I knew was doing the same thing. I was nearly six feet six high, and had the mind of a fairly bright child of twelve.

I shared a small round tent with eleven other men. One was a painter named Paul Nash, with whom I became great friends. Before long I realized that I was inconveniently tall for the trenches, and I applied for a commission in the flying branch of the Navy. However, the Admiralty would not commission me until the War Office had released me, and the War Office would not release me until the Admiralty had commissioned me. This depressing stalemate was suddenly ended by the intervention of Private Nash. He gave me an introduction to a friend of his called Eddie Marsh, who was Private Secretary to the First Lord of the Admiralty, Winston Churchill.

On a sunny day towards the end of April, 1915, I presented myself at the Admiralty, and clumped selfconsciously into a magnificent room with a high window overlooking the Guards' Parade. I clicked the heels of my muddy marching boots, saluted, and stood stiffly to attention. l had never, until two days earlier, heard of Eddie Marsh. I saw a dapper man of about forty, in an elegant grey suit, with a grey silk tie of a slightly lighter shade. He held himself upright, making quick movements like a bird. And when he spoke, it was with a bird's voice. The pitch was high, and very slightly nasal. When he was excited or amused, he twittered like a bird. His eyes were bright, and his bushy eyebrows swept upward into points, like a genial Mephistopheles. His ears, I noticed, were the only ears I had ever seen, except my own, which were perfectly flat, having no curl on the outward edge.

But the thing that caught my attention most was his monocle. He used it to punctuate and emphasize what he said. It was indeed *part* of his conversation. He used to screw it into his eye at a certain point, and then later, with great effect, open his eye very wide and allow it to drop on to his waistcoat at the end of its black cord.

'So you are Paul's friend,' he said, smiling at me.

'Yes, sir,' I replied in a parade-ground voice.

'Well, you seem to be in an impasse' ; he made a little bright gesture : 'We must see what we can do.'

'Thank you, sir !' said Private Sieveking.

Eddie gave his head a rapid sideways tilt : 'I think that Paul excuses us from the formality of "sir" ' he chirped, and let his monocle fall, thus abolishing 'sir' for good.

Somewhat shyly I stood myself at ease, and then 'easy.' In spite of his cheerful, almost gay, manner, there was a something—a shadow every now and then in his eyes, the reason for which I understood before long. He had just heard of the death, on active service, of his dearest friend, Rupert Brooke.

Looking back, I have always felt that, on that day in April, 1915, Eddie was already looking for someone to fill the place in his life left suddenly empty by the loss of Rupert Brooke, and that he greeted each new man he came across hopefully. If so, he was, in my case, disappointed. It was years before he met Christopher Hassall, the young poet who to a great degree was able to take Rupert's place.

But whatever was in Eddie's mind that afternoon, we went out for a stroll in the sunshine and, taking my arm, he began to tell me about Rupert Brooke. Round and round the Guards' Parade we walked, Eddie reciting first one poem and then another in his own unforgettable, unforgotten way. He had a 'Period' voice, with those beautifully articulated late Victorian and Edwardian cadences, and special pronunciations and emphases of certain words, never heard today except from very old gentlemen. It is a manner of speech that has almost entirely passed away. His friend Neville Lytton had it to perfection ; and another of his friends, Bertrand Russell, has it too. It is not in the least degree affected. It is a perfect expression of distinguished personality, most delightful to listen to.

> '*Ah God ! to see the branches stir*
> *Across the moon at Grantchester !*
> *To smell the thrilling-sweet and rotten*
> *Unforgettable, unforgotten*
> *River smell, and hear the breeze*
> *Sobbing in the little trees. . . .*'

Eddie's voice quivered slightly ; he paused and looked away across St James's Park ; and there was a silence. Then, after a great business with the monocle, he resumed, and did not show any emotion until nearly at the end. The bird-like voice had in it a fierce, almost harsh overtone when he came to :

> *'Deep meadows, yet, for to forget*
> *The lies, and truths, and pain ? . . . Oh, yet*
> *Stands the Church clock at ten to three ?*
> *And is there honey still for tea ? '*

Less than a fortnight later, Asquith made the cardinal error of requiring Winston Churchill to resign his office as First Lord of the Admiralty. During his last few days Churchill must have signed scores of papers of all kinds, many of worldwide importance. But one was of greater significance than all the rest—to me. I like to think that his very last act before leaving the Admiralty on his last day was to sign that shimmering, that miraculous document: the memorandum which gave a commission as Flight Sub-Lieutenant R.N. to Private L. de G. Sieveking.

* * * * *

When a famous man dies, all manner of people come forward and tell what they remember of him. Some knew him when he was eight, some when he was eighty, and some in the years between. He himself has probably written an autobiography. All are essential if a truly stereoscopic portrait-in-the-round is to be created. In looking at a man, no two angles are *quite* the same, and every individual 'shot' adds a fraction to the portrait.

On January 13, 1953, the death was announced of Sir Edward Marsh, K.C.V.O., C.B., C.M.G. It sounded merely as though one more elderly gentleman who had survived from the Edwardian era had ceased to breathe. But a number of people were able to pull aside the pompous disguise that was trying to merge him indistinguishably among the vast and ever-growing company of honoured mediocrities. For to them it was 'Eddie' who had died—Eddie, whose highly developed individuality stands out against the background of twentieth-century England, lit by a serenely mellow and entirely personal spotlight. . . .

He had a gift for friendship with people of all sexes, and of all ages. And though he was eighty when he died, two years ago, there are plenty of people still alive, many of them quite young, who have their own unique memories of him.

*   *   *   *   *

This is not the place for anything except my own personal memories of Eddie. But I feel I ought to give a few of the bare facts of his life. He was born in 1872. His father was Howard Marsh, Professor of Surgery at Cambridge. One of his great grandfathers was Spencer Perceval, the Prime Minister who, in 1812, was shot dead in the lobby of the House of Commons. Parliament voted £50,000 as compensation to his family, and a little of this trickled down to Eddie, who used it to help the young artists and poets among whom he had so many friends.

When Eddie left Westminster and went up with a scholarship to Trinity College, Cambridge, he met and became friends with many people, among whom were Maurice Baring and Bertrand Russell. He entered the Civil Service in the year I was born, 1896. Four years later, in 1900, he became Assistant Private Secretary to Joseph Chamberlain. In 1905 he became Winston Churchill's Private Secretary, and he remained with him until the middle of 1915, going with him to the Duchy of Lancaster Office after the resignation from the Admiralty. This only lasted a few weeks until Churchill joined his regiment at the front.

I have before me, as I write, a letter from Eddie dated November 17, 1915, from his bachelor chambers at 5, Raymond Buildings, Gray's Inn, in which he says:

'. . . *The P.M. is taking me on as an extra Private Secretary, which I consider as falling as nearly as possible on my feet, after the shock of breaking my 10 years association with Winston. . . .*'

In the next letter he says:

'. . . *Winston is back for a few weeks' leave. He's been having very narrow escapes, but is extremely fit and loves his regiment. I believe he's very popular. . . .*'

*   *   *   *   *

Eddie had three worlds: his professional Whitehall world; the world of artists, poets, and stage people; and Society with a capital S, now vanished. But one thing at a time. An ineluctable fact is that during the best years of his life he was always a private secretary. To Joseph Chamberlain, Winston Churchill, Asquith, the Duke of

[60]

Devonshire, J. H. Thomas, Malcolm Macdonald. And being a secretary, however exalted, does something to you. You have to subject your personality to that of your master. It becomes second nature to you to think, not as yourself, but as your master's secretary ; during professional hours at any rate, to react to people and events, not entirely as yourself, but as a loyal, and often admiring, secretary.

I hadn't realized this until I read Eddie's quasi-autobiography, *A Number of People.* It was published in 1939, but I didn't read it until just after his death. I was startled. I had always wondered what must have been Eddie's feelings on becoming secretary to Asquith, who had forced his beloved Winston to resign. But this book gave me an entirely new view of him.

I seemed to sense again a subtle flavour that I had tasted in, for example, the book on Bernard Shaw, written by his secretary, Miss Patch, just after Shaw's death. But with a difference. Eddie had an immense diversity of other fields beyond his professional life, out into which he burst, full of vigour and zest, the moment the duties of Whitehall had been done for the day.

But even in these other circles he sometimes seemed not altogether to have cast off the life-long habit of service to another's personality. Perhaps this accounted a little for his extreme modesty, his almost excessive tact, his willed blindness to faults in other people.

But nothing could repress his enthusiastic appreciation of the good things of life, his humour, and his kindness of heart. He enjoyed good talk, wit, good food, the company of beautiful women, and clever women. And in 1911 he began to buy, with the little money at his disposal, the work of young painters whom his discriminating taste told him were worth encouraging.

One day in the summer of 1915 I got some leave and went, for the first of many times, to stay with Eddie at Gray's Inn. I didn't know anything at all about modern painting, and had never seen the house of a collector. I climbed the stairs to his front door on the second floor —or was it the third ?—and was let in by his faithful housekeeper, Mrs Elgy.

I looked round the hall, and through the open doorway of a room. Everywhere, from floor to ceiling, were paintings. As I followed her down a passage into the room where Eddie was awaiting me, I was overwhelmed with shyness. During luncheon the monocle flashed and glinted as the urbane, graceful phrases pleasantly chirruped out after

D

each other in the air above the delicious food. After luncheon he took me round his collection.

He had an odd little mannerism of leaving sentences unfinished, which came into play on occasions when special kindness, extra tact were necessary ; when, in fact, he wanted to conceal the other person's shortcomings from him. This was emphatically one of those occasions. We went from room to room, every wall completely covered, doors hung with paintings, paintings leaning against chairs.

He murmured : 'This little Sickert. . . . you like it ? . . . I've always thought it rather . . .'

And a moment later : 'Stanley Spencer. I bought it at the Carfax Gallery. Do you think I was wrong ?' and then, letting his monocle fall, 'I thought it rather gay, and . . . Mhm . . .'

But the height of eloquent omission was reached when we peeped into Mrs Elgy's bedroom. This too was completely hung with paintings but she had hung her dresses over some of them. Eddie pursed his lips in vexation.

'I do *wish* . . .' he said.

We inspected the lavatory and the bathroom. And their walls too were covered with pictures.

But I, like the couple in the poem, 'said nothing all the time.'

It was in the theatre that Eddie really blossomed out with all his exuberant zest. The discrimination which enabled him to pick out at their beginnings painters like Paul Nash and Duncan Grant, who have since become world famous, deserted him in the theatre. At First Nights he was like a schoolboy. He revelled in it all. Two remarks, heard one evening before the curtain went up, describe him exactly.

James Agate : 'Now then, Eddie, you can't be enjoying it already !'

Arnold Bennett : 'Eddie is a m-miserable fellow. He enj-j-joys *everything* !'

One night he took me and the girl I was in love with at the time to the first night of a show in which Ivor Novello had written some of the songs. We walked down the Strand to the theatre, and Eddie sang us a new song that had taken his fancy.

> '*K-k-k-katie, K-k-k-katie !*
> '*You're the only g-g-g-girl that I adore !*'

His stylish, *fin-de-siècle* pronunciation of the word 'adore' is quite impossible to render in print.

We were in a box provided by Ivor. Just before the curtain went up, Eddie leaned towards us and whispered : 'If you don't like it, don't say anything.' He could not bear to hear criticism of any of his friends. But his letters often contained anecdotes such as the following. At a First Night, *Frank Curzon . . . came round in front, in hopes of hearing praise from the audience. The only thing he heard was a woman saying to another "Well, dear, you would come !" . . .'*

It was not only young painters that he loved to encourage, but young poets also. His anthologies which appeared between 1911 and 1922 under the title *Georgian Poetry* contain many names now famous, such as Rupert Brooke, Walter de la Mare, and D. H. Lawrence. He was vexed when I told him years later of a verse of Brooke's in a letter to another private secretary at Number Ten, in which the phrase occurred :

> *'Oh, I have eaten haggis meringue*
> *'And strange ambiguous bun. . . .'*

It should, he felt, have been included in the Memoir.

This same private secretary, when I was having tea one day at Number Ten in the secretaries' room, told me how someone had once asked Eddie what he'd done with a certain document :

'I am *certain* I put it in the War Office out tray,' he replied seriously. *'I remember the gesture.'*

Eddie reminded one of those charmingly urbane figures who used to throng Holland House in its great days. In some ways like a character from Proust's densely populated pages, he knew 'everyone' in Edwardian Society—and out of it. Every week-end he stayed at one or other of the great country houses that existed in those days. As a universally welcome guest, a patron of the arts, and as a writer of entertaining letters, he was in a way like Horace Walpole. A difference was that he was not a rich man with utter freedom to develop his own personality.

He loved the society of young people of all sexes, and nothing made him happier than when he was able to encourage and help them in practical ways. Many of his young friends were gifted in one way or another, but I had absolutely nothing to recommend me to his friendly notice. Above all, I had no social gift.

Yet he used to take me to dine with the Winston Churchills, in— was it ?—Eccleston Square ; and with Lady Randolph Churchill, where we were waited on by female footmen in pale blue tail coats. I hope I was not as much of an embarrassment to Eddie as I was to myself as I sat at the tables of the mighty, bursting with physical health, very tall, in appearance somewhat like a young horse, bright crimson in the face, a picture of agonized shyness in my sparkling new naval uniform. I was a sort of male version of the proverbial 'dumb blonde.' The only explanation of Eddie's continued friendship then, and during the years that followed, was his pure generosity of heart, and his unfailing loyalty when once his friendship had been given. . . .

I have sometimes wondered about Eddie and sex. He was nearly forty-three when I met him, and it seemed to have no place in his life. But I fancy that he must once have been 'a bit of a lad' in an elegant and rather correct way. The only positive clue I have is contained in one of his letters to me :

'. . . I do envy you your new-found power of enjoying your past. I haven't got it a bit. So long as I'm on the same page in the book, I love thinking back the earlier lines of it, but once the leaf is turned the previous pages bore me a little, partly because I'm ashamed, both of what I was, and of having changed, (which is a bit inconsistent !) . . .'

How should one interpret that ?

*   *   *   *   *

There is much more I could write about Eddie, but I will conclude with an odd little incident that took place on what he said was the happiest evening of his life.

On March 17, 1937, a group of Eddie's friends gave him a banquet to celebrate his knighthood. Winston Churchill was in the chair. When all the speeches were over everyone began to stroll about. Emboldened by wine, I went and sat down for a moment beside Mr Churchill, and told him that, though I was a Liberal as he had once been, what I looked forward to more than anything else was his becoming Prime Minister.

Mr Churchill smiled, patted me on the arm in a fatherly way, and replied :

'You never will, my dear boy. It's too late. They don't want me. I shall *never* be Prime Minister.'

And Eddie, who came up at that moment, leaned over us with monocle flashing, and murmured Asquith's often-quoted admonition : 'Wait and see !'

MARTYR LOVE

THE LIFE OF LAURENCE OLIPHANT

by PHILIP HENDERSON

XCEPT PERHAPS for his novel *Piccadilly*, an unexpectedly savage attack on Victorian high society of the 'sixties, the name of Laurence Oliphant is now almost forgotten. Yet, like other contradictory characters of this age of contradictions, Oliphant was driven by self-dissatisfaction, boredom, and a hunger for excitement and adventure into strange paths. His name is continually cropping up in the diplomatic history of the nineteenth century, for wherever there was a crisis in the affairs of the world Oliphant was to be found. He also shared to a considerable extent in one of the more fantastic religious manias of his day.

At thirty-six, in 1865, when he finally surrendered himself body and soul to the American prophet Thomas Lake Harris, Laurence Oliphant was on the threshold of what promised to be a brilliant diplomatic career. True, his only official appointment had resulted in his nearly being killed four years earlier in Japan after ten days at his post. But he had also been to China with Lord Elgin in 1857 and his *Journey to Khatmandu*, written during a trip through India to Nepal as a very young man in the company of Jung Bahadour, is still one of the most readable of Victorian travel books. Subsequently he traversed Russia from St Petersburg to Sebastopol and, as luck would have it, the Crimea War broke out just after the publication of his *Russian Shores of he Black Sea*, which went into four editions in six months. Another book, *Minnesota and the Far West*, resulted from a year spent as Elgin's secretary, when the reciprocity treaty between Canada and the U.S.A. was 'floated through on champagne.' Undoubtedly, Laurence Oliphant was one of the most widely travelled, politically knowledgeable and charming young men of his time. And when he met the Prince of Wales in Vienna in 1861 the Prince, like everyone else, fell beneath the charm of his conversation. 'He sugar-doodles the ladies,' was the comment of his Royal Highness afterwards.

It was in fact Oliphant's popularity with the ladies that led to his downfall—he confessed that he wanted to possess a thousand, though there is no means of knowing whether he achieved this operatic ambition. But on his return from the Far East he evidently gave himself up for a time to the pretty free life of the man-about-town. Indeed, one sometimes wonders why the Victorian age should ever have been called prudish when we learn that the Haymarket, with its eating-, drinking- and meeting-houses, blazed with light till dawn, and the whole area south of Piccadilly to the river teemed with night houses and Turkish baths of the most questionable character. Here young swells used to resort, after bandying inanities, in lavender gloves and white ties, with the young heiresses of Mayfair and Belgravia. 'Most people are, I suppose, more or less conscious of leading a sort of double life—an outside one and an inside one,' Oliphant writes at the conclusion of his picaresque *Episodes in a Life of Adventure*. 'The more I raced about the world, and took as active a part as I could in its dramatic performances, the more profoundly did the conviction force itself upon me, that if it was indeed a stage, and all the men and women only players, there must be a real life somewhere. And I was always groping after it in a blind sort of way—not likely, certainly, to find it in battlefields or ball-rooms, but yet the reflection was more likely to force itself upon me when I was among murderers or butterflies than at any other time.'

It was this persistent concern with his inner life, and the search for 'reality' behind the glittering façade of the Victorian social and political world, that made Oliphant such an easy prey for Thomas Lake Harris, when that prophet was in London delivering his sermons in Wigmore Street in the early sixties. In his strange novel *Masollam*, written after he had broken with his former master, Oliphant gives the following picture of him :

> His hair, which had been raven black, was now streaked with grey, but it was still thick, and fell in a massive wave over his ears and nearly to his shoulders, giving him something of a leonine aspect. His brow was overhanging and bushy, and his eyes were like revolving lights in two dark caverns, so fitfully did they seem to emit dark flashes, and then lose all expression. Like his voice, they had a near and a far-off expression, which could be adjusted to the required focus like a telescope, growing smaller and smaller as though in an effort to project the sight beyond the limits of natural vision. . . .

Harris was, in fact, a good showman and, as an ex-Swedenborgian minister, knew well how to impress his hearers. At the conclusion of *Piccadilly* he appears in person to exhort Lord Frank Vanecourt and his companion to 'Live the Life.'

Before accepting him into the Brotherhood of the New Life, Harris tried to make Oliphant marry his mother's maid, whom he had 'wronged.' This he refused to do, though he was prepared to give up everything and follow Harris into the wilderness. He had at this time just been elected to Parliament as Liberal member for Stirling Burgh, and great things were expected of him. Unfortunately Harris forbade him to speak in the House ; otherwise he was to continue living his life as before until the Call came, except that, as a discipline, he was to devote a certain amount of time each day to mending petticoats— surely a command not without irony !

The Call was not long in coming, after Harris had satisfied himself that both Laurence and Lady Oliphant were prepared to make all their property over to him, and Laurence and his mother were given permission to sail to Amenia, New York, where Harris ruled as complete autocrat over a small community of dedicated souls. On their arrival, Lady Oliphant was put to housework and Oliphant was directed to live alone in the loft of a cattle shed, where he was to sleep on a straw pallet on the floor and make his own furniture out of vine boxes. During this 'probationary' period he was not to speak to anyone and his work was to consist of cleaning out cattle sheds and currying horses, for Harris maintained that a return to nature and an association with animals might purify him of the evils of civilization. Then, for days at a time, he wheeled barrows of dirt and rubbish, as a symbolical punishment. Later, he worked as a farm labourer under two Irish navvies. This was designed to humble him and give rest to his brain. And Oliphant, who had taken the 'Use' name of Wood-bine, said that he had never been nearer to Christ in his life, and that Amenia was not only a new life to him, but the beginning of life itself.

During the summer of 1867, Harris moved the community, or the 'Use' as it was called by its members, to a new site at Brocton, largely on money provided by the Oliphants, though they were not consulted and Harris continued to treat them as servants. The community was more than self-supporting, for Harris conducted a flourishing grape-growing business not only on the money provided by his adherents but by their labour as well, for they all felt as though they were working in the Lord's vineyard. Harris himself sat in an inner sanctum and was seldom seen. Here he wrote long epics at the dictation of Blake, Byron, Shelley and Keats and fought terrible and solitary battles with the black forces for the souls of his flock, which left him prostrated for days. He also left his body and visited distant stars. Occasionally, a particularly favoured member—usually a young woman—was admitted to the presence for 'consolation.' And having regard to the main articles of the Harrisite faith, expressed with such admirable concision by the master himself in the following lines :

> Soul-life and sex-life are at one,
> In the Divine their pulses run.

there can be little doubt about the form this 'consolation' took.

Apart from 'open breathing,' a form of Yoga, and celibate marriage, the principal article of this strange faith was the doctrine of counterparts, each person having somewhere in the universe his or her spiritual mate. The counterpart did not, as a rule, inhabit the body of one's husband or wife, but it might sometimes be found in the body of another member of the opposite sex ; and, as union with one's counterpart was the aim of life, this belief led naturally enough where it might have been expected to lead. But Harris was extremely strict in such matters, where other people were concerned, and usually the counterparts of other members of the 'Use'—at least in its earlier days—remained tantalizingly incorporeal. Only Harris, who was the most advanced spiritually, might from time to time discover more material counterparts. The principal 'caretaker and consoler' of the community, however, was Harris's heavenly counterpart, the Lily Queen, and 'consolation' from the Lily Queen was only to be found, logically enough, in the arms of Harris himself.

It is hardly credible that Oliphant, with his wide knowledge of men and affairs, should have been imposed upon by this sort of thing. But Harris was such a powerful personality, with such hypnotic powers, that he induced the most intelligent people to accept his views and to believe in him implicitly. Moreover, he could convince them that he alone of all the community at Brocton was in direct contact with the Deity. Many wealthy and dissatisfied people came to him, begging to be eased of the responsibility of their money ; to poorer people he was more difficult of access ; the really poor made him feel quite ill, and after contact with them he retired to a sort of vomitorium where he washed out their influence. He suffered as acutely from contact with people who did not believe in him.

After a time it occurred to Harris that Oliphant might be more usefully employed on various business enterprises for the benefit of the community. In 1870, however, he was allowed to return to Europe. Harris had no objection to his joining the staff of *The Times* as correspondent in the Franco-Prussian war, provided that practically all the money he earned by his labours should return to Brocton.

It was while he was living in Paris with his mother in 1871 that Laurence Oliphant met and fell in love with the charming and highly intelligent Alice Le Strange. He had to get Harris's permission before he could marry her, of course, and this was by no means easy, for doubtless the prophet sensed in Alice a rival in dominion over his most distinguished and useful follower. But at last he consented, on condition that Alice made over all her property to him and that the relations of husband and wife should be entirely under his control. Alice Le Strange and Laurence Oliphant were then married at St. George's, Hanover Square, and returned to live in Paris, where they were left in comparative peace by the master for a year—except that, as they lived in accordance with the Harris doctrine, their marriage was strictly celibate. And this for Oliphant was particularly difficult, as he was now passionately in love. He described their wedded state as 'martyr love,' which, he said, was so necessary if the steady undermining of the principle of selfish love was to be achieved, and he learnt self-control by sleeping with his 'adored Alice' in his arms without ever consummating their marriage.

When the Oliphants returned to Brocton in 1873, they found the prophet in a difficult mood. First of all, he directed that Alice should be buried up to her neck in the earth. 'Perhaps you can become fit to dwell among us, if the right means be used,' he said. 'We shall see.' She was then put to do housework along with Lady Oliphant and to look after the chickens. It was essential, said Harris, that her 'much admired refinement, polish and intellectual charm' should be put off. Her husband he sent away on business to New York. All this Oliphant bore patiently. But worse was to follow. Harris moved to California, taking Alice and a few other particularly favoured members with him. Lady Oliphant was left washing handkerchiefs at Brocton, while Laurence worked away for the community, visiting England and travelling about Europe. After two years, he went to California, hoping

[69]

to see his wife again, only to be sent away with bitter reproaches. For Harris, it seems, had begun to discover in Alice distinct resemblances to his heavenly counterpart, the Lily Queen.

Peculiar rumours now began to reach the outside world of the life Harris was leading at Fountain Grove, California, and when Oliphant and his mother went there they found their worst fears confirmed. The initiates of California had thrown off all restraint and had begun to find their celestial counterparts in one another's arms without let or hindrance, Harris having built an 'arch-natural' house, to facilitate such discoveries, in which the beds of the sleeping quarters were arranged in recesses round the walls of one large circular room.

The shock was too great for Lady Oliphant, and she sickened and died. Alice meanwhile had left the community and was supporting herself by teaching. And then Oliphant himself fell seriously ill. The scales had at last dropped from his eyes and he authorized the friends who were nursing him in San Francisco to begin proceedings against Harris for the recovery of at least part of the money he and his mother had invested at Brocton. The rift between Harris and his disciple was now complete, and when he received the first lawyer's letter he cabled to Alice to join with him in taking steps to have her husband certified as insane. It was then that Alice Oliphant awakened to the real nature of the man for whom she, too, had given up everything.

Yet, though disillusioned in Harris personally, the hold of his strange beliefs still remained, and in 1882 the Oliphants went to live in Palestine, where they instituted their own mystical cult of the heavenly counterpart. Together they wrote *Sympneumata* from mediumistic dictation, a book which sought to impart a doctrine of 'high love' between men and women, who were seen as bi-sexual, the woman being the centre of the man and the man the 'circumference' of the woman, and they believed that the world would be transformed and mankind saved by this revelation. 'Mr Oliphant's idea was that the sexual passion was the only real spiritual life,' wrote the Philadelphia Quakeress Hannah Whitall Smith, who spent years investigating various forms of religious fanaticism, 'and that in order to be spiritually alive you must continually keep that passion excited.' After a lifetime of martyr love, Alice Oliphant now devoted herself to imparting sympneumata to the Arabs. 'No matter how degraded and dirty they were,' writes Mrs Smith, 'the contact of her body brought about, as she supposed, the coming of the counterpart. It was a great trial for

her to do this, and she felt that she was performing a most holy mission.'
A number of people from England joined the Oliphants in this holy
work at Haifa until their activities were finally stopped by the National
Vigilance Association and the Turkish government.

Alice Oliphant died of a fever in January, 1886, after a trip to Lake
Tiberias, which Oliphant described as the happiest fortnight of his life.
But her death was only a temporary interruption of their relationship.
At first it seemed to Oliphant absolutely impossible to go on living
without her, when 'suddenly one night the light seemed to burst
through, and she came to me so radiant, and at the same time so sad at
seeing me unhappy, that my grief seemed to be lifted by the effort she
made to dispel it.' From that time he continued to feel her more and
more. 'She seems sensationally to invade my frame, thrilling my
nerves when the sad fit is on,' he wrote, 'and shaking me out of it.'
In fact, his whole frame used to shake and shudder convulsively with
these visitations. 'She is very busy with you,' a friend remarked, as she
watched Oliphant writhing on the sofa. Alice was able to reach him,
he said, 'through the internal tie which had been formed by this
interlocking of our finer-grained material atoms while in the flesh.'

During the last two years of his life, Oliphant had something of the
appearance of the Ancient Mariner, with his grey glittering eyes and
long grey beard, and indeed he had a wonderful tale to tell. In the
autumn of 1886 he was invited to Balmoral to expound sympneumata
to the Queen. He wrote his racy memoirs, *Episodes in a Life of
Adventure*, another novel *Altiora Peto*, which might be described as the
work of a Victorian Aldous Huxley, and a strangely confused exposition
of his religious theories, *Scientific Religion*, an amalgam of spiritualism,
atomic physics, theosophy and Harris's *Esoteric Science*. Unfortunately
the practice of sympneumata had its dangers. A young American
widow, studying art in Paris, was so shocked by the liberties Oliphant
began to take with her, while expounding his creed, that she lodged
a complaint with the National Vigilance Association, who thereupon
prepared a case against him for corrupting the morals of the young.

But it was in the summer of 1888, staying once more in Paris on his
way back from Palestine, that Oliphant was shown a letter from
Rosamond Dale Owen, the grand-daughter of Robert Owen. He at
once set off for New Harmony, Indiana, determined to meet her.
Rosamond, herself a well-known spiritualist, had already had
intimations of his coming. All her life, she says, she had prayed for 'a

stately mate,' and shortly before Oliphant's arrival she began to prepare her trousseau. She was not deceived, for Oliphant asked her to accompany him back to England, where they were married. 'Do not be troubled, dearest friend,' he said to her, 'you are not beautiful, it is true, but through you, Alice seems to be more intimately restored to me.' It was to be martyr love for Rosamond, too. The day after her marriage the wife became the nurse. Oliphant fell seriously ill with cancer of the lungs. 'Just in time he came to me,' writes the second Mrs Oliphant in her book *My Perilous Life in Palestine*, 'so that I might tend him to the end, with Alice's help, for I had the strength of two women.'

Laurence Oliphant died at Twickenham, after a few months of illness, that same year. With a look of exaltation on his face, softly humming snatches of 'Safe in the arms of Jesus,' he passed peacefully away. Some weeks later, he returned to Rosamond with the message 'Death is delicious,' and, in spite of threatening letters from the National Vigilance Association, who had now perforce to drop their case, she returned to Palestine to carry on her husband's work among the Arabs. The second Mrs Oliphant lived till the age of ninety, after the closing of the Oliphant centre at Haifa, and was buried in North Wales in 1937 in the birthplace of her grandfather, Robert Owen.

THE WAY OF ETHEL M. DELL

by NANCY SPAIN

ETHEL M. DELL is the true romantic, the novelist whose very name is synonymous with passion. Passion is always nice. But that is not the whole secret of Ethel's perennial appeal. She died in 1939, in her fifties, but her works are all still in print. And a fortune has been made out of her most famous title, *The Way of an Eagle*, alone.

This wonderful book was turned down by eight publishers, one of whom considered it 'nothing out of the way.' It found its way eventually to the now extinct firm of Fisher Unwin. Tom Werner Laurie, their manager, who was later to make a fortune of his own with two imitation Ethel M. Dells (Victoria Cross and Joan Conquest), 'thought it might do for the First Novel Library.' Even Tom thought so little of it that the contract drawn up agreed that the first 500 copies should be sold without benefit to the author. He was gambling quite heavily in publishing the work of an unknown woman. Before 1912 Ethel had only written serials for the magazines. The booksellers, of course, had never heard of her. And the booksellers refused to order *The Way of an Eagle*. Then Tom Werner Laurie thought of announcing it as 'The Novel with an Ugly Hero.' The reading public (who are never wrong) were fascinated. From a little trickle of library orders the demand became overwhelming. *The Way of an Eagle* soared to success. And so did Ethel M. Dell.

By Christmas of 1912 Fisher Unwin had exhausted twelve editions of *The Way of an Eagle*, selling a million and a half copies in so doing. And it is still as well-loved as ever. In 1954 it reached its sixtieth edition.

Why does a book succeed like this? You may well ask. If authors knew they would obviously sit down and do likewise.

First and foremost, Ethel wrote with passionate, unswerving sincerity. She really believed in her characters : her ugly, fascinating army officers (all her men are fascinating and 'marred' in some way) her beautiful, wronged women (her women are always beautiful and nearly always wronged), her cads (her cads are more caddish than any other cads in fiction).

Second, when her characters spoke, they spoke in character. They used the sort of language that we all understand. They even swore. 'Damn!' they said . . . even if they had to apologize for it later.

Third, something *tremendous*—like a seduction, or a kiss, or an unmasking of a coward and a poltroon—took place on every single page, sweeping her readers off their feet, gasping and panting, until the end when the hero and heroine look at each other 'with fire and memory and understanding in their eyes.' (This is the last sentence of *The Way of an Eagle*.) Whenever I pick up an Ethel M. Dell I always say 'God bless her.' She really knows how to tell a story.

Do you remember the story of *The Way of an Eagle* ?

Muriel, our heroine, has taken to eating opium on the sly because she is the daughter of a General of a besieged garrison somewhere in India. She eats the opium because she gets so terribly depressed and it is the only way she can pass those sleepless nights. The General, her father, knows that he is doomed and he tells one of his subalterns— Nick Ratcliffe—to escape, taking Muriel with him through the mountains. . . .

Now Nick, our hero, as Tom Werner Laurie spotted all those years ago, is terribly ugly. He has a face like a yellow mask, all puckered and wrinkled up. He has a grin that leaps 'goblin-like' across his face from time to time. He has eyes 'like a snake charmer.' But in spite of all these terrible physical disabilities he is full of character and fight. And the General knows quite well that only Nick, out of all the Regiment, has the character to take his beloved Muriel to safety.

They have *awful* adventures on the mountains. Muriel (who is half-drugged half the time, poor dear) awakes from a swoon to see Nick fighting like a mad thing with a mountain tribesman who has attacked them. Nick is strangling the mountain tribesman with a terribly bestial look on his face . . . so she is terrified of poor old Nick from then on.

Eventually they get back to safety and Muriel stays with a Mister Will Musgrave and his wife Daisy. Daisy is a weak character who has been in love for some time now with a man who is not her husband : Blake Grange (big, powerfully built, with absolutely marvellous thews and things) got the V.C. fighting in the siege that Muriel and Nick ran away from.

Well, Nick and Muriel have been through much together. And they have a quick, short-lived engagement, exchanging a ring that says 'Amor Vincit Omnia.'

But Muriel can't bear the memory of the way Nick looked when he strangled the tribesman. So she disengages herself.

Somewhat surprisingly she then gets engaged to Blake Grange, V.C. She doesn't know, you see, that Blake would be so silly as to love a married woman. 'It was unthinkable,' says Ethel of him, 'that the giant frame and mighty sinews could belong to a personality that was lacking in corresponding greatness.' Weak is Blake, terribly, terribly weak over his love for Daisy.

The scene changes rather abruptly to England, England rocked (as always) by tempests and bad weather and storms and all that. After a bad landslide on his land Nick sees Daisy and Blake wandering together on the foreshore, wooing and kissing and carrying on regardless. I suppose they think they are unobserved because before the landslide there was a bit of cliff in the way? Anyway, Nick is furious. He knows that Daisy is untrue to her husband, while Blake is obviously not good enough for Muriel. So, after a stormy scene when everybody's eyes flash (and Blake is terribly weak), *that* engagement is off.

Then, somehow, they all get back to India again (perhaps they have been on leave?) and Nick dresses up as a beggar in a *chuddah* and asks for rupees outside the residency. Why? So that he can get an occasional glimpse of Muriel, of course. That is why he is standing by when Muriel is attacked again.

> She never fully remembered afterwards how she came to realise that Nick—Nick himself—was there before her in the flesh, fighting like a demon, fighting as she had never seen him fight since long ago, when every nerve in her body had been strung to agonised repulsion . . .
>
> She felt no repulsion now—no shrinking of any sort, only a wild anguish of fear for his sake that drove her down the intervening steps like a mad creature, that sent her flashing between him and his adversary, that inspired her to wrench away the smoking revolver from the murderous hand that gripped it . . .
>
> She went through those awful moments as a woman possessed, blindly obeying the compelling force, goaded by sheer primeval instinct to protect her own. It was but a conflict of seconds, but while it lasted she was untrammelled by any doubts or hesitations. She was superbly sure of herself. She was superbly unafraid.
>
> When it was over . . . she sank down on the steps, a trembling hysterical woman, and began to cry . . .

That is an Ethel M. Dell woman all over. Tomboys to the backbone while the battle is on, they play mixed hockey and gallop madly to hounds with the rest. But after primeval passion has seized them in its awful grip, down they sit on the Residency steps and have a jolly good sob.

Muriel longs to tell Nick she loves him. But she can't find words.

'My dear girl' says Nick. 'In Heaven's name don't try. Words were not made for such occasions as this . . . They are clumsy tools at the best of times. You can make me understand without words. I'm horribly intelligent, as you remarked just now.'

So, after the tumult of Muriel's emotion has swelled a bit, she snatches Nick's hand and presses her lips 'closely, passionately upon his open palm.' And they get married and go for a frightfully uncomfortable honeymoon in a tent in a ravine in Kashmir. And live happy ever after.

What a book. What a story. Can you wonder that Ethel M. Dell is my favourite authoress? What a woman she must have been to write such marvellous stuff. Who was she? What was she like?

She was born on August 2, 1881, the second daughter of Mr and Mrs John Vincent Dell, of Ashford, Middlesex. (Mrs Dell had been a Miss Parrot before marriage.) Her father was from India, a fine military type of man. Ethel, too, was tall : she was about 5 feet 10 inches. Mrs Sylvia Douglas, 'a junior in the Post Office in Ashford in those days,' remembers her well. 'She was somewhat pale, grey-blue eyes that seem to look right through you, beautiful teeth and when she smiled her face just lighted up.' She dressed plainly : in a costume and shirt blouse 'as the fashion then was' and when she went out she rode a bicycle.

Mrs Douglas also remembers the excitement over the manuscript of *The Way of an Eagle*. Handwritten from end to end (Ethel never used a typewriter), it was sent off to Fisher Unwin by 'hand express,' and when it was accepted for publication 'printed cards' were sent as well. That manuscript is now in the British Museum.

Ethel married in 1922, for love, Colonel Gerald Savage, D.S.O. They met in Guildford at Colonel Savage's sister's : for dinner. He saw her come downstairs 'and there was never anyone else.' They went to Cornwall for their honeymoon. They were undisturbed, but only because Col. Savage had the military foresight to leave Guildford in the early morning before the reporters could get at them from London, travelling pseudonymously as Mr and Mrs Gerald White in a very small motor car. And they cut all the name tapes out of the bride's underclothing.

Ethel was probably the shyest authoress in the world. The Garbo of English Literature, she refused to allow any photographer to take her picture, any sly newshound to interview her. She was intensely religious, she gave away thousands to charity. After her great success her income became about £25,000 a year. She gave up her bicycle and drove about in a large plum-coloured Rolls Royce. A white Samoyed dog called Henry usually sat beside her. Invariably a Union Jack fluttered on the radiator cap. She was so intensely patriotic she would allow no American movie company to make a film of one of her books.

She wrote over twenty-seven books. And these books are all so well loved that librarians will tell you they are never on the shelves. But there are still some sad snobs who think her work is 'tripe.' Ethel M. Dell was well aware of this. She says so in her novel, *The Juice of the Pomegranate*. And one morning when St John Ervine reviewed one of her books rather unkindly, complaining that he supposed that sort of thing sold : Ethel came down to breakfast laughing heartily.

'What a pity for poor St John Ervine,' she said,
'That he finds it all so un-nerving
    That stuff written by Dell
    Should sell and should sell
When *his* is so much more deserving.'

And she must have also have had a good laugh at lovely copper-haired Diana, wild and tomboyish heroine of *The Juice of the Pomegranate*. Diana is the step-daughter of stern Sir John Carvis and weak Lady Carvis. She has gone to stay in London with Blanche, her sister. Blanche is a young married woman who gives bridge parties. Her house is very neat. There is a prim parlourmaid and Diana finds it all too, too terribly correct and boring for words :

. . . She finished her cake and drank some more tea with the vigour of a vast contempt. Then, in the act of taking another cigarette she caught sight of a book, just protruding behind a cushion, and pulled it out.
'Hullo ! Here's a find. Now we shall see what the brainy Blanche reads in her leisure moments. Something she's none too proud of obviously ! Great Scott ! It's an Ethel M. Dell.'

E   [77]

Incidentally, Diana has a terrible time in London, and she is betrayed by an awful man with little glittering slit-like eyes, who turns out to be Sir John's horrid stepson. She won't let him anywhere near her. That is why he puts drugs in her drinking water and why the book is called *The Juice of the Pomegranate*. But before all this happens she has a thundering good row with Blanche. Blanche is rather a bore. She says :

> 'I think that the real sequence (in a love affair and marriage) should be first the dream, then—the fulfilment, and after that the awakening. That is the true way of happiness.'

Diana receives this with a wild harsh laugh.

> 'Did you get that out of an Ethel M. Dell novel ?' she says. 'I did see a book by that most contemptible of all novelists hiding under a cushion in this very room the day I came, and I just wondered. It's a good thing I didn't read it or my literary taste might have been vitiated for ever !'

Diana then remarks that she will put the Ethel M. Dell novel where all her sister's highbrow friends will 'mark and learn—even if they refuse to read.' She says it will 'be a terrible exposure, but it will damn well serve Blanche right.'

It has always seemed to me as though Diana had never read one of Ethel's books. People who have never read them are always loud in their condemnation. At one time there was even a rumour that they had been banned in H.M. Female Prisons. My mother always told *me* that they had an inflaming influence upon the young. Utter rubbish, of course. Ethel M. Dell was always on the side of truth and light. She was a master story-teller, a genius. In her lifetime, in spite of the sneers of people like St John Ervine, many people claimed to be her 'ghost writer.'

The most notorious of these spurious ghosts was Mrs Jackson, victim of the famous Forged Papers Murder Case.

'I never quite knew who Mrs Jackson *was*,' said Mr Jackson, accused of murdering her in a Mumbles bungalow. 'Sometimes she even said she was Ethel M. Dell.'

THE MISSING MONARCHS

by MICHAEL HARRISON

EFORE THE LAST WAR, I worked in a London publisher's office, and there in the stock-room I would often encounter a visitor, who seemed to have some business with the packers.

He was a man somewhat unusually dressed, and the eccentricities of his apparel were such as to make our honest Cockney packers laugh. The visitor took all this highly personal amusement in good part, and though I never did discover why he called on the packers, and not on us—the Editors—I got to be able to recognize a curious quality in the packers' laughter, and to know when he had chosen to visit us.

Gerald Kersh has noticed this odd character in one of his books, but I may briefly describe him once more.

He was thin, blue-jawed, sunken of eye, and he wore his dark brown hair in ringlets which lay upon his sloping shoulders. On this rather tangled profusion of hair he bore what used, in my youth, to be called a 'tammy' (something quite different from a beret)—a 'tammy' of wine-coloured velvet or velveteen, matching, in its sombre tint, that of the long monastic robe he wore. His naked feet were sketchily sandalled, and in the front of his 'tammy' he wore a very inexpensive-looking diamond star.

He was, said the packers, the Rightful King of Poland. And That was why he wore Them Robes. (And that Star, said the apprentice. That's right. And *that* Star.)

'Ask him, why don't you?' said the Head Packer. 'He'll tell you, just the same he told us. Won't he, Jim?'

There was no need to ask. Not long afterwards, the gentleman got his name into the papers, and the story came out.

Since then, I have met several Rightful Kings, and I have sufficient acquaintance with the class to be able to divide it into two : those claimants of whose right to the claim there may be no doubt ; and those whose claim not everyone admits. I am casting no doubts on the right of the robed gentleman with the long hair and the tammy to call himself King of Poland ; but it is not a right that everyone concedes him. On the other hand, no one—not even Tito—would deny to King Peter the right to call himself claimant to the throne of Jugoslavia.

Yet it is only fifty-two years since Peter's grandfather arranged for the brutal assassination of the then King of Servia—Alexander Obrenovitch—and his queen, Draga. These two unfortunates were dragged from their beds in the royal palace at Belgrade, and cut down with the cavalry sabres of the murderers. Peter's grandfather, Peter Karageorgevitch ('Black George's son') then ascended the throne.

In those days, governments had to *pretend* to have a conscience, whether they possessed one or not. The British Government could do no less to express its abhorrence of this dastardly crime than break off all relations with the new *régime*. In fact, it was only Peter's happening to be on the side of the Allies in 1914 (as things turned out, he could hardly have been on any other side !) which ended the diplomatic rupture. Eleven years after what has been politely called the 'Belgrade coup,' Peter found himself a 'gallant little Ally.'

Still, as I say, no one would dispute the present Peter's right to call himself claimant to this fifty-two-year-old monarchy.

Old Peter, indeed, was a man whose ambitions deserved better things. At the end of the war which his own obstinacy had begun he not only absorbed much of the territory of defeated Austria, but double-crossed his brother monarch, Nicholas of Montenegro, even though Peter had married Zorka, Nicholas's daughter.

Nicholas, whose royal dignity dated only from 1910, had made some wonderfully impressive alliances for so unimportant a monarch. His son, Crown-prince Danilo, had married the daughter of Adolphus Frederick, Grand-duke of Mecklenburg-Strelitz (then a sovereign state federated within the German Empire) ; one daughter, Militza, had married His Imperial Highness the Grand-duke Peter of Russia ; while another, Anastasia, married, first, His Imperial Highness George Maximilianovitch de Beauharnais (descendant of Napoleon's Josephine, by her earlier marriage), 5th Duke of Leuchtenberg and 3rd Prince Romanovsky, and, second, H.I.H. the Grand-duke Nicholas Nicholaievitch of Russia. A daughter, Helen, became the gentle, self-effacing, kind-hearted Queen of Italy ; and Princess Anna of Montenegro, the fourth daughter, married Prince Francis Joseph of Battenberg, and is thus the distant relative of both Lord Mountbatten and his nephew, the Duke of Edinburgh.

Only one of these connections could have helped Nicholas of

Montenegro, when his kingdom was threatened by his son-in-law, Peter of Servia. But the Italians, though they were on the winning side in 1918, were not disposed to exert any pressure to save Nicholas's throne. His small state was annexed by the Servian king and added to what was taken from Austria, to make up the new federated 'Kingdom of the Serbs, Croats and Slovenes.' The theft of Montenegro was solemnly approved by the Conference of Ambassadors which assembled at Paris on July 13, 1922.

Nicholas, poor man, retired to that Sargasso Sea of dethroned monarchs, the Riviera, where he died on March 1, 1921. His son, Crown-prince Danilo, 'succeeded' him, but 'abdicated' on March 7 following, in favour of *his* son, Prince Michael (born 1908). This prince lives mostly in Paris or Italy, and it is known that he bestows the Order of Danilo the First on favoured acquaintances, and such strangers as have exerted themselves in the Cause of his restoration to the throne. In the meanwhile, King Michael of Montenegro is in the same position as that in which his might-have-been-neighbour, King Michael of Roumania, finds himself : a monarch without a throne.

They are not the only ones.

How many are there ? I made a rough count before I set out to write this article, and I calculated that, within the past five centuries— say, from the fall of Constantinople, in 1453—no fewer than a thousand reigning sovereigns have been forcibly deprived of their sovereignty. The figure, indeed, may be much higher than that ; for there are odd little flash-in-the-pan sovereignties, such as that which raised the red flag of Algiers over both Lundy and Iceland (yes—Iceland !), about which the details are hard to gather. And, too, there are the 'regencies' of generals fighting on after the central governments have collapsed : such men, as in the case of Alexander's generals, always set up 'sovereignties,' and often these become permanent.

What happened to the Emperors of Constantinople ?

When I was a very young man I met a 'rightful Emperor of the East' ; but I am still doubtful of his authenticity. Yet, though it is true that the last Emperor, Constantine XI (or XII, by some reckonings) was killed, and that a junior branch of the imperial Palaeologus family, lords of Monferrat from 1305, became extinct in 1533, the family of Palaeologus did not become altogether extinct even in 1533. One of the family—Maurice—was French Ambassador to St Petersburg in the fateful year of 1914, and died as recently as 1944, a very old diplomat of eighty-five. And I have met some English country gentlemen bearing the name.

But the romantic legend has it that the Palaeologi closest to the succession fled from Constantinople, and came to that first-settled of all English districts, Cornwall, where they changed their name (but not much) to Constantine. Two centuries later, they were given grants of land in the Somers Islands, in the Caribbean, and there they settled down again, as West Indian planters.

These planters gave their name to their slaves, and so the descendant of one of these slaves bears the famous name—that he has made more famous in modern estimation : Learie Constantine.

Another branch of the Byzantine imperial house had made themselves Emperors of Trebizond, and Trebizond lasted seven years longer than Constantinople, before the Turks swept the Christian throne away and replaced it with a Moslem Emirate that the Soviets have only just abolished—thus adding one more to our list of throneless monarchies.

And, since we are in that part of the world, let us not forget the family which was dispossessed by the father of the present Shah of Persia : the family of Kadjars. His Imperial Majesty Sultan Achmed Shah Kadjar, Shah-in-Shah, who was born at Tabriz in 1898, and succeeded his father on the Peacock Throne in 1909, was deposed by Riza Khan Pahlavi, who had judiciously played the French and the British off against each other, and got them both to save his throne from the Bolsheviks, attacking under Kirov (who was later assassinated).

The ex-Shah went, almost as a matter of natural law, to live in the south of France, where he was forgotten until he brought a libel action against a French newspaper who had cracked a (French) joke about 'La nuit, tous les chat sont gris'—'By night, all cats are grey'— but which *could* sound like : 'La nuit, tous les *Chahs* sont gris'—'By night, all Shahs are tipsy.' He died in 1930, at Neuilly-sur-Seine, but he did not die, in the phrase of the genealogists, *s.p.m.* He has heirs, and many people must have wondered why a 'rightful Shah of Persia' did not pop up at the time of the Abadan oil crisis. Perhaps he did, and perhaps . . .

Still, let us get back to throneless kings. Zog—who, like Napoleon III and Napoleon I, rose to be a king from a president—was last heard of leaving the United States of America, where there was some dispute with the Federal income-tax authorities.

Perhaps he, too, dreams of recapturing the throne from Enver Hodja, the friend of Russia? But then, what about *another* rightful occupant of the throne of Albania : Carol Victor Wilhelm Friedrich Ernst Gunther, Prince of Wied, born 1913, who succeeded his father, Prince Wilhelm of Wied—the 'Mpret'—on the 'throne' of Albania?

Prince Carol does not, it must be admitted, call himself King of Albania. He is officially listed as merely 'Crown Prince,' but his sisters are all styled 'Royal Highness.'

For that is the trouble with abdications and forced exits : one's successor may also leave in a hurry, and so you have, with Albania, what you have with Spain and France and Afghanistan and Mexico, and several more : a duplication of 'rightful heirs.' Oddly enough, in the case of Prince Carol of Wied, he has two 'rightful claims' : one to the sovereignty of Albania, and the other to the sovereignty of his own hereditary estate of Wied. But of that presently.

There is, by the way, another who has a claim to two thrones : Abdul Medjid Effendi, Caliph of the Faithful, who has successfully married his family into more stable Moslem monarchies. Abdul took over as a 'limited monarch' when Mustafa Kemal Atatürk expelled the Grand-sultan Mehemet Vahid Ed-din Khan VI in 1922. The Sultanate was abolished by the Turkish National Assembly, but the Caliphate remained, and it was to the vacant Caliphate that the Assembly elected Abdul. Then, in 1924, Abdul was deposed in his turn, and since then he has been spending his time on the Monarchical Grand Tour, between Cairo and Antibes, and cementing family relations with other members of the Moslem Bloc. He was born in 1868, but he has been married four times—the last time, in 1921, to a lady who is still only fifty-two.

There are plenty of heirs to contest Abdul's claims in the future.

Besides, they have *two* claims : to the Grand-Sultanate-with-Caliphate, and to the Empire of the East ; for when the Byzantine Emperors were overthrown in 1453 by the Turks, the Sultan did not—as is too often thought—abolish the Roman Empire of the East. He took it over, calling himself *Keisar-i-Rûm*, and retaining, on his standard, the crescent and star which were the badge of the city of Byzantium. On the other hand, since a niece of the last reigning Christian Emperor of Byzantium married King Ivan III of Russia (so that the Russian monarchs came to call themselves 'Imperator' because of that fact, and also made themselves Supreme Heads of the Orthodox Church), doubtless the Russian royal family have a claim to Byzantium. Though, of course, Ivan was not a Romanoff . . .

Talking of that, the present head of the Romanoff dynasty, and Pretender to the Russian throne, is His Imperial Highness the Grand-duke Vladimir of Russia, son of the Grand-duke Kyril who died in 1938, in France. Vladimir was born in 1917. His father married a grand-daughter of Queen Victoria.

But Vladimir, in his personal relationships, has done something to heal a long-standing dynastic breach by marrying Princess Bagration, whose brother is the present pretender to the throne of Georgia.

It may well be that this claim, should it ever come to the practical test, might be disputed by the heirs to smaller Georgian states which were dispossessed by Russia at various times between 1800 and 1867. The principal unit of the loosely federated union of kingdoms and principalities called 'Georgia' had been taken under the protection of Russia at the end of the eighteenth century. The Persians, under the fierce Agha Muhammad, attacked and burnt Tiflis. Georgia appealed to Russia, who preferred not to help, but later, with the assistance of the pro-Russian princes, Orbeliani, Tumoshvili and Chavchavadze, took over the Bagratid Georgian kingdom in 1800. The kingdom of Mereti put itself under the 'protection' of Russia in 1804, and was annexed in 1810.

The same pattern followed with the states of Samskhe, Guria, Svaneti and Abkhazin : the states were 'protected' and annexed ; the dynasties were deposed. At last, only the Principality of Mingrelia was left. It, too, had a treaty of 'protection' with Russia. But, in 1867, the Prince of Mingrelia abdicated and made over his throne to Alexander II—sometimes called the 'Liberal Tsar.'

Of course, the abdication was not voluntary, and the heirs of Mingrelia have reason for holding that an abdication extracted under duress is no abdication at all.

The Prince of Mingrelia was only twenty when he submitted to Russian pressure. 'Invited' to Petersburg, he lived there until 1903, when he died, still only fifty-six. For his brother, Andrey, he had obtained the dignity of Prince of Mingrelia in the Russian peerage, with the style of Most Illustrious Highness. For other members of the family he got the style of Prince (or Princess) Dadian. There are plenty of heirs, and we may hear more of Mingrelia.

To revert for a moment to the Russian Pretender : his youngest sister, H.I.H. the Grand-duchess Kyra Kyrilovna, is married to Prince Ferdinand of Prussia (grandson of Big Willie, and thus the present Prussian Pretender). Ferdinand is in trouble now, because of a rumour —which does not seem to be with much foundation—that he has been associating with Dr Otto John.

Vladimir's record is excellent. He was imprisoned by the Gestapo, but refused to become a German puppet. In this respect, he differs strikingly from another dispossessed monarch, H.R.H. Nicholas Friedrich Wilhelm, Grand-duke of Oldenburg, of the same family as the royal house of Norway. H.R.H., whose father, the Grand-duke Friedrich Augustus (died 1931) abdicated—with the rest of the German sovereigns—in November 1918, was one of the earliest Nazis, being *S.A. Standartenfuehrer* and commander in the '*S.A.-Reiterstandarte 14.*' Naturally, he joined the Nazis 'under duress,' as his father abdicated under duress. So nothing final has yet been done. Nothing to alter the essential *rights* of the dispossessed . . .

It was in Germany, a century and a half ago, that the greatest number of claimants was made at any one time.

From the (real) foundation of the Holy Roman Empire in 962, by Pope John XII and the Emperor Otto, until 1806, something over six hundred 'sovereignties,' big and small, were loosely federated within the Empire.

In 1804, the Emperor (of the Holy Roman Empire) Francis II, fearing that Napoleon I was about to take away his imperial title, announced that, in future, he would be the Emperor of *Austria-Hungary*, and two years later Francis formally dissolved the Holy Roman Empire. The year was 1806.

The German princes, now without a symbol-head, met in the Diet which had always been the real source of their federalized authority, and decided—most of them—to put themselves under the protection of a new emperor—Napoleon.

The great man rewarded them : duchies became grand-duchies ; grand-duchies became kingdoms ; titles were exalted, and even the junior members of merely 'comtale' families found themselves entitled to be called 'Durchlaucht'—'Serene Highness.'

What was even better for the princes, Napoleon anticipated the remark of his nephew, Napoleon III, and said (in effect) : 'Gentlemen : help yourselves !'

Those states—including Wied—which were merely 'mediatized' were lucky. 'Mediatization' means that, where before they held their feudal fiefs immediately of the Emperor, they now held them indirectly —through some greater vassal. That was the idea, the fiction. In effect, the 'mediatized' states were deprived of their sovereignty. There were fifty of them.

But, as I said, they were luckier than most, including the Prince-bishopric of Wurtzburg, which shared the fate of the Archbishopric of Cologne and the Republic of Venice. Nearly six hundred 'independent sovereign states'—sometimes they were hardly more than a walled townlet—were shared among the more powerful members of what had been the Holy Roman Empire.

As soon as Napoleon began to do badly, the German princes seceded from their alliance with the Emperor, and, calling themselves the Germanic Confederation, summoned their first independent Diet, at Frankfort-on-Main, November 16, 1816. They did not, however, when they gave up Napoleon, give up the territories or titles that he had bestowed upon them ; and even the Austrian Emperor revived an Order of Chivalry which had been founded by the Corsican : the Order of the Iron Crown.

During the nineteenth century Prussia removed the sovereignties of Hanover—whose king was a Prince of Great Britain and Ireland (and who made the usual 'reservation' of all his rights, later)—Hesse-Cassel, Frankfort-on-Main, Nassau and Schoenburg-Hartenstein—thus leaving 33 independent sovereign states in the German Empire (including five free cities).

With the wholesale abdications of November, 1918, the 28 personal sovereignties were added to the claimants' list.

Take Roumania, now. It is a modern state, formed of the two principalities of Moldavia and Wallachia. Michael, the ex-King, is a Hohenzollern, and 'rightful king.' But before the two principalities were welded into one, and a Hohenzollern put over them, first as Prince (subject to Turkey) and then as King, the twin principalities were ruled by the Ypsilantis and the Ghykas. The families are still extant, still titled Princes, and still very much in the swim. Neither has a 'rightful claim' to Roumania, as a whole, but each has a claim to one of the parts from which the united kingdom of Roumania was made. Shall we hear from them ?

When we think, too, about the tendency of claimants to multiply, we may reflect upon the fact that no fewer than forty persons claimed to be that small son of Louis XVI who was supposed to have died in the Temple prison, during the French Revolution. One of the claimants was a free-lance American missionary to the Indians. His claim was taken so seriously that the Prince de Joinville, son of Louis-Philippe, actually went to see the man, and had a long interview, from which the Prince, they say, emerged 'looking very thoughtful.'

Nor must we forget what we may call the 'impersonal' sovereignties, which are real enough, even though it is rather a group than a single individual who is claiming rights. There is more than one exiled republic, though the chief is, of course, the Sovereign and Military Order of Malta, whose Grand-master—'acting regent'—ranks after cardinal-deacons, and ranks, too, as a prince, by concession of Austria and Italy, with the style of 'Most Eminent Highness.' This republic-in-exile (for Napoleon took their island away, and Britain took it away from Napoleon, and forgot to return it to the Order) still enjoys considerable autonomous rights, sending its own diplomatic representatives to several states—but not to Britain !

Florence, too, has not forgotten that, as late as 1847, it was one of the three sovereignties—Austria and the Vatican were the others—which recognized (and thus legitimated) the claim of the several descendants of Stanislaus II Poniatowski, last King of Poland. The City of Florence made the then head of the family Prince of Monte Rotondo and a Patrician of Florence. Austria made him Prince Poniatowski, the Vatican legitimated him, and the French Empire made him a French subject.* The third Prince and his brother, perhaps thinking that the throne of Poland might be some time in returning to the family, married two American ladies : Miss Elizabeth Sperry, of Stockton, and Miss Maud Goddard, of New Brighton, U.S.A., respectively.

And, of course, we can hardly think of Napoleonic France and the U.S.A. together without thinking of the American Bonapartes : descendants of Jérôme Buonaparte (later King of Westphalia) and Elizabeth Patterson. This marriage was held to be valid by Napoleon III, and the children of the union legitimate, though not in the Line of Succession. This ruling, though, could be disputed.

One thing that I have noticed in my researches into royal claims is

* Because Prince Walewski, son of Napoleon I, was French Foreign Minister at the time.

this : that royal families seem to show a surprising survival-quality, once they are away from the cares of office.

The family of King Theodore of Corsica (that unlucky monarch who was imprisoned in the Fleet Prison) seems to have died out : the family name was Neuhoff. The elder branch of the Bourbons became extinct with the death of the Comte de Chambord, on August 24, 1883. The Count could have become King Henry V of France, in 1871, but he would not consent to the use of the tricolour, even though it was proposed to 'seme' the white part with fleurs-de-lys. So France has had a republic ever since. (All the same, the Count of Paris is back in France.)

Senior Reuss is extinct, and a few—a very few—others. But most of the other claimants are well supplied with heirs, direct and indirect.

I cannot trace the descendants of David de Mayréna, King of Sedangia. And I cannot trace the son of James de Harden-Hickey and his wife, daughter of Flagler, the oil-king, who built Palm Beach.

Harden-Hickey made himself Prince James I of Trinidad, and nearly started a war between Britain and Brazil. He shot himself in El Paso, Texas, in 1898, but left his principality in trust for his son.

Amanullah, they say, is still in Rome.

But I miss an old acquaintance, the King of Redonda, whose poet-laureate is 'the rightful Emperor of Mexico.' The King of Redonda will always be remembered by me for a letter that he once wrote, and which was headed :

From Our Court-in-exile,
—, Coptic Street,
London, W.C.1.

There breathes the whole indomitable spirit of CLAIM !

LIZZIE: MY LANDLADY

by FRED BASON

TEN YEARS NOW I've been writing in this annual, and most of the time have written about myself. This year I want to write about someone else—my faithful friend and greatest fan, my ever loyal housekeeper, Liz.

Over the years I must have had at least five hundred letters and postcards asking me why I've never married Lizzie. Let's get that cleared up. Lizzie is a good deal more than twenty years older than me. She's a grannie five times over, and very proud of it! We have stayed together through genuine affection, true respect, and the fact that it suited the two of us.

Ours was not an accidental or even a romantic meeting. Lizzie, who was born, like myself, in Walworth, has known me all my life. There has always been Lizzie somewhere in the background. Some twenty-five years ago she and her son and daughter came to live in the top flat of 152 Westmoreland Road, S.E.17, where I lived downstairs, with my own people. Lizzie had been a widow for a long time. I lived a lonely and rather unhappy life, for my parents were over forty when I was unexpectedly born, and I always felt (and was sometimes told) that I wasn't wanted.

Upstairs there was always a welcome for me, and the kind of encouragement a young chap wants. Time went by and Lizzie's son and daughter left home to get married. Lizzie, who had a bad heart, retired with a little pension. There she was, always upstairs, alone.

One day my mother said to me : 'Fred, you're upstairs so often you might as well stay up there.' Without a moment's hesitation I took up my goods and chattels. Lizzie gave me one of her rooms and became my landlady. Two lonely folks found in each other's company the solution to a lot of problems. From that day to this I've never regretted it. Almost all I am I owe to Lizzie. At least four times through the years I'd have died if it hadn't been for her.

Let's go back and try to fill in the picture of this good and brave and genuine Cockney.

Lizzie never went to school. She was taught her ABC by her own daughter, when the said daughter was just fourteen. Letter-writing is a great and grave task for her, and I have to be at her side to spell even the simplest of words. But in a year she writes to at least fifty *Saturday Book* readers, who have heard about her through me.

Lizzie's mother died when she was seven, and Liz had to be mother for her sister age six and brother age four. Her dad was a jobbing free-lance printer, travelling around with three children and a great liking for wallop. Liz says she was very very often hungry.

The years went by and Lizzie married. Again came tough times, when she was left a widow with two children under four to bring up and not a shilling capital behind her. Having no trade and no education—just a weak heart—she was forced to take any job that would keep body and soul together. She became a ladies' cloakroom attendant. Long hours and little wages . . . long hours in a badly ventilated basement. Often and often she was on duty 14 hours a day. She had that job for twenty years !

Now allow me to describe her. She is just under five foot two. Weighs a little less than seven stone. Is very slim and neat and fragile . . . rather like a Dresden china figure when she's all dressed up. Her real name is Mrs Elizabeth Keep, but if you called her that she'd say: 'You ain't Royalty—is you ? I'm Lizzie.' There is nothing starchy about Liz and although at times very famous folks call upon me (and I best say here that our 'At Home' day is *Thursday*) dear Lizzie soon breaks down formal barriers, and everything is all friendly like —as, for instance, when Ruth Draper came to tea and Lizzie said in a loud whisper : 'You can see as how she's a *real* lady because she keeps her hat on for tea !'

Ruth Draper never fails to ask after Lizzie every time we meet. Once she sent Liz a food parcel all for herself, but Liz shared it with all the neighbours. She'd share her last shilling (my last shilling) with anyone in need.

Liz is very superstitious. You could never get her to walk beneath a ladder or pick up a fallen knife. She couldn't put a shoe on a table or touch spilt salt unless she threw it over her left shoulder. Never will she empty her teacup till she has explored her fortune in the tea leaves.

If the morning is wet she doesn't say it's raining. 'The angels are crying,' she says : 'Some one did wrong last night.' Or, if it's a sunny morning : 'The angels are smiling. Good was done yesterday.' She talks of death as 'God's welcome.'

On October 20 last year I came into the room just too late to hear the opening of the six o'clock news so I asked Lizzie if there was any news. 'Oh, the Queen has given Mr Eden her garter, or something,' says Liz. 'I wonder what Mrs Eden will have to say about that ?'

But she isn't by any means as slow as you might think. Here's one of her sayings, straight out of the blue : 'All men are on the look-out for a dream woman. Meanwhile they gets married.'

When she wouldn't believe there was a real person called Lady Docker, because only *men* work at the docks, I showed her a photo of Lady Docker in a newspaper. 'Docker's not a name ; it's an occupation,' says Lizzie ; 'Lady Regal would be a better name for *her*.' And, after a minute or two : 'Then she'd be a picture palace !'

Politics isn't Lizzie's strong point. She has always voted Tory, but only because the local Tory candidate is a man she respects. 'He looks as though he'll do something when he's got something to do.'

Her favourite man of the world is Alec Clunes, the actor, 'He talks so lovely,' says Liz, 'Hearing him talk so nice is worth the price of the ticket.' On January 5 this year Alec Clunes sent Lizzie the largest box of chocolates she'd ever seen in her life. She took hours to pen her thanks—must have torn up twenty pages before she got the letter how she wanted it. No gift can ever have given anyone more joy. One chocolate a month is her ration, and I don't doubt there's still some left in the box as you read these words.

She's also a fan of Frank Pettengell, the character actor—'He looks so comfortable ; you sort of feel he wouldn't take a part unless he could do it all proper.'

Jane Wyman and Kirk Douglas are her film favourites. The kind of film she likes is 'one you can get into as one of them—not like a stranger looking in.'

On the radio she likes Bernard Braden, Ted Ray, Tommy Trinder and Susette Tarri. And whenever the announcer ends off a programme by saying 'Harry So-and-So is appearing at the Palace Theatre,' Lizzie adds, 'All the rest are out of work and wish they too were appearing with Harry So-and-So even at the Battersea Power Station.'

One thing that annoys her on the radio is the studio audiences, turning on their laughter and applause like a tap. I've told her how helpful a studio audience is to a performer. 'Let them take their mothers-in-law,' says Liz, 'Then they'll get a *real* opinion.'

She's never seen a play by Shakespeare or read a book by Dickens. One evening I gave her a volume of Keats to look at. It sent her to sleep. When she woke up she said : 'Don't he use a lot of funny words ! He gets nowhere ever so fast.'

One Sunday afternoon I was walking through Nelson Square, off the Blackfriars Road, when I saw a plaque on a house saying Shelley lived there once. When I got home I told Liz how much I'd like to live in that house. 'Don't Shelley live there any more ?' asked Lizzie. 'No, dear,' says I, 'he don't live there any more.' 'Oh,' says Liz. 'Perhaps he's moved to the L.C.C. flats round the corner.'

When I took her to a classy first night Lizzie nodded her head at some women in very low-cut gowns who were going into the theatre ahead of us and said : 'They look as though they was going in for a good wash instead of a good play.' And, seeing some gentlemen in tails she said : 'Take after their ancestors, don't they ? *They* had tails, too.'

Once when I was in funds, after doing a radio series, I asked Liz if she'd like me to take her abroad. She's never been outside England, not even to Wales or Scotland. 'No, I'd rather not,' she said. 'Why ?' I asked her. 'Because I'd meet such a lot of foreigners,' she answered.

Lizzie's never seen a professional golf, tennis or cricket match. But she gets worked up to wild excitement over a big fight on the radio. And she has a system of backing horses which makes a steady little profit year after year. With her permission I'll pass it on. She bets on horses whose last three placings have been third, second, and then unplaced. She says : 'Tried once, got a place. Tried again, nearly got there. Then a nice restful outing. Next time he'll win.' And he does—for Liz.

Lizzie's greatest joy is a deckchair on the sands of a crowded seaside resort. She isn't one for the country. 'Nothing to see but fields. And I'm not a cow.' But she loves flowers and she loves to potter about in the little garden we've got, no bigger than a good-sized dining-table. She's real pleased if anything she's planted is allowed by the cats to come up.

All through the Blitz Lizzie stayed in London, forever bright and cheerful. Golly, the times *I* was frightened ! But Lizzie was unmoved. A bomb destroyed half of her home, but nothing touched her spirit. 'Foolish man, that Hitler. Not guts enough to have a real go. Not sense enough to give up before he's caused a commotion.'

Although our life together has been more successful than most marriages Lizzie says she'll be real happy when she's seen me married. I know—and she knows—I'm no use on my own. 'Have two children,' she says to me, 'and if one of them's a girl I'll be happy if you'll kindly call her Lizzie.'

The
Saturday Book

ANNALS

OF

SPORTING

ARCHERY AT HATFIELD, 1792. *Engraving after Richard Corbould*

THE ROYAL TOXOPHILITES

Text and photography by VICTOR MITZAKIS

NOT SINCE the Battle of Agincourt has England had as many toxophilites as she has today. In 320 clubs throughout the country some twelve thousand enthusiasts devote their spare time to the booming sport of archery. The oldest of these clubs is the Royal Toxophilite Society, which has its grounds on the site of the old Tyburn burial ground within a bowshot, as it were, of the Marble Arch. During the season, which ends in October, members meet regularly to don the Lincoln Green of tradition and practise an art which has a hallowed place in the history of England.

Rapidly gaining popularity as a sport, archery has not always been the pleasant pastime it is today. The time was when the Long Bow was the weapon of England ; effective legislation made it so, for the Statute of Winton (1275) obliged every man to own and use a bow and, amongst other things, laid down that he would practise on all Holy Days. It was this type of legislation that made the English bowman the finest in Europe and enabled him to win resounding victories at Crécy, Poitiers and Agincourt. The introduction of the Cross-Bow and subsequently of the Arquebus caused the decline of the Long Bow as a weapon, but as a sport archery continued to flourish, and excepting the period between James the Second and George the Fourth all English monarchs have been patrons of the sport. The chronicles of Henry the Eighth shows him to have been an enthusiastic archer and an inveterate gambler on the results of the competitions ; he is reputed to have created a dukedom for one of the archers of his bodyguard who won a tournament.

The Royal Toxophilite Society, which is to archery what the M.C.C. is to cricket, was formed about 1770. In 1792 the Prince of Wales, later George the Fourth, laid down what became known as the 'Prince's Lengths'—that is, shooting distances of 100, 80, and 60 yards—and prescribed the scoring values of the target ring as : Gold 9, Red 7, Blue 5, Black 3 and White 1. Other clubs began to appear, and by 1844 the sport had become so popular that in that year was held the first Grand National Archery Meeting open to all British archers, an event which has been held annually ever since, with the exception of the war years of 1939–45. Today British archers compete in all the main international competitions.

It may seem strange that today so many people are being attracted by this primitive yet singularly difficult sport. It is possible that deep down in the British character there is an inherent interest in the bow, the weapon of their forefathers. A more practical explanation is that archery is a sport for all ages and both sexes, great physical strength not being essential. It is, moreover, an inexpensive sport, and its social scale ranges from the jealously guarded preserves of the Royal Toxophilite Society to the more humble but equally competent small county club.

The modern bow has as much in common with its predecessor as has the rifle with the musket ; today, thanks mainly to American research and influence, the bow is a precision instrument made either of new type laminated woods or of steel. Arrows, again under American influence, are of light alloys and are made by specialists to the closest tolerances ; the wooden arrow is obsolescent.

The beginner's equipment, consisting of a bow with a pull of 30 pounds, together with six arrows and a bracer and tab to protect the fingers and fore-arm against the lash of the bow string, can be had for as little as £10.

Much envied by his English cousin, the American archer is not restricted to target shooting ; special hunting laws allow him to pursue the exciting sport of Bow Hunting before the hunting season proper commences. Amongst the great exponents of this branch of archery is the fabulous Howard Hill, who is reputed to draw a bow of 170 pounds and is admittedly the greatest field archer in the world today. This wider application of the sport probably accounts for the greater development of modern archery in the United States.

There is perhaps a salutary lesson to be drawn from the fact that the bow and arrow, known as a lethal weapon since the dawn of recorded history and used as an instrument of warfare until comparatively recent times, has now become, through its numerous enthusiasts all over the world, a means of bringing to its exponents a mutual ground of common interest and thus furthering international friendship.

The illustration opposite is of Mrs J. K. Flower, Lady Champion of England

On the right Mr Frank Bilson, who is President of the Southern Counties Archery Association and an international bowman, demonstrates the leather 'bracer' and 'tab,' which protect the fingers and forearm against the whip of the bow string. The bracer fits round the forearm, the tab on the fingers. Below, Mr Bilson shows the correct position at full draw, and at the foot he illustrates 'nocking'—the action of putting the bow string on to the arrow. In the close-up below Mrs Flower shows the arrow 'nocked.' The knot on the bow string is termed a 'kisser,' and when the bow is fully drawn it should touch the lips.

The photograph on the opposite page is of Commander W. N. Drawbridge, R.N., a member of the Royal Toxophilite Society.

Mr. Frank Bilson, in the grounds of the Royal Toxophilite Society, demonstrates 'stringing' —bending the bow to attach the bow string.

Target bow at full draw. A normal bow has a pull of 50 lb. A hunting bow is deadlier than a .303 rifle.

Correct stance at full draw. A copy of the early English Long Bow, of which no original specimen exists.

A laminated modern competition bow. Yew bows are still used, but are giving place to the American bow of duralumin.

posed photograph showing the arrow
ginning its flight. A beginner's arrow costs
All arrows must bear the archer's name.

The arrow has just left the bow. The
archer observes its flight. Arrows are
numbered and must be shot in order.

The stance for 'Popinjay' shooting, with a
pecial blunt-nosed arrow—a sport which
s mainly practised on the Continent.

A long-range shot. The longest recorded
flight of an arrow is 975 yards. In recent
years an American has shot 700 yards.

The club house of the
Royal Toxophilite So-
ciety is in Albion Mews,
north of Hyde Park. The
Society, whose Patron is
the Queen, conducts its
competitions with a mini-
mum of publicity. The
targets, 48 inches in diameter, consist of five
coloured rings, the centre
being termed the 'Gold'
and counting 9 points,
against red's 7 points.
The most coveted prize is
the Six Gold Badge,
gained by shooting six
consecutive arrows into
the Gold. Only two lady
archers have gained this
since 1905. The highest
rating an archer can get
is that of Master Bow-
man: there are only
nine in England.

PLEASURES OF CROQUET

by RAYMOND MORTIMER

TUPIDLY I CONTINUE to be surprised when I find that my friends do not know even the rules of Croquet. From my earliest years I remember the click of balls on the lawn, interspersed with eager talk about rushes, split-shots, the next player, taking two off and pegging out. But then I was a child when Croquet was at the zenith of its popularity.

No, I am not a centenarian. The heyday of the game was not during the Crimean War but in the opulent reign of King Edward VII. Then there were tournaments, over a hundred of them, all over England and Ireland. Guests would arrive to stay in country houses bringing their mallets, as now they bring their tennis-rackets or golf-clubs. The ladies wore special shoes with bridges of leather joining the sole to the high heel, but these were seldom visible under the long skirts trailing over the grass behind the players. No player ventured a step out of doors without a hat : the sun was considered lethal. Ladies protected themselves with long white gloves, and—except when they were actually making a shot—they carried sunshades. Beneath these, and above billows of puffed out hair, there were hats the size of the largest salvers, supporting Still Lifes of roses, pansies, violets and carnations. The men wore straw hats (never known then as 'boaters,' so far as I can remember), or Homburgs (green felt hats with a ribbon bow not at the side but at the back), or, if they were very dashing, panamas. The game would be interrupted by tea in a summer-house— silver pot and urn, cake-stands with three tiers, one of them certainly proffering seed-cake. This supposed delicacy has not come my way for thirty years, I am glad to say, and I suspect that it has vanished like the veils that were twisted under the chin and pushed up to the nose when seed-cake was eaten.

Make no mistake : none of these paraphernalia interfered with the skill of the players or the rigour of the game.

'Shall I shoot, partner ?'

'Wiser, don't you think, to go to the corner.'

'Before laying the break for you shall I make the last hoop, or leave you to peel me ?'

Thus would run the considered debates upon tactics. Croquet, perhaps I should explain, is a game of positions, like billiards and chess. You must try to leave your opponent so situated that any move he makes can be turned to your advantage. Once you have all four balls placed just where you want them on the lawn you should be able to make as many hoops as you wish without any stroke that demands exceptional skill or luck. But an experienced opponent will make it very hard for you ever to get the balls thus ideally situated ; and, even when you have succeeded in this, any inaccuracy in one stroke makes the next one correspondingly difficult—which always happens if you cease for an instant to concentrate.

A cool head is therefore essential : loss of temper makes concentration impossible. My childhood memories do not include the alarming (or delicious) spectacle of a grown-up in rage, smashing his mallet or bringing it down on his opponent's head, which is supposed to be a usual event at Croquet. In my experience paroxysms are far more frequent at golf. Nervousness rather than fury is the besetting temptation on the Croquet-lawn.

Croquet-players are believed to be muffish as well as peppery. (The game, I understand, has even been rechristened 'Lawn-Billiards' in Australia, where men are so manly that they seem terrified of appearing the reverse.) On this point my defence will be different. By all means call Croquet muffish, for I claim this as one of its principal advantages. As we grow older, are we to play nothing but Bridge or Canasta ? (Cards, incidentally, are, for some reason, never dismissed as muffish—nor, for that matter, is Bowls.) How delicious to find an outdoor game at which your handicap does not automatically grow longer as middle age advances. One can take up Croquet at forty and expect to make steady improvement. It is possible to win the championship at sixty.

The 1914 War destroyed the popularity of Croquet. Doubtless many private lawns could not be maintained because there was a shortage of gardeners (the motor-mower, I suspect, was then a rarity, if indeed it existed). But when peace returned, there should have been no difficulty in restoring Croquet-courts at any rate in all the clubs. I suspect that the game went out because it was thought slow : this was the Jazz Age. Everyone, moreover, wished to seem and to feel young : old ladies wore skirts that did not reach the knee. Croquet was dismissed as a dull, dowdy affair, and the bad name it then received still obtains.

Most of the odd notions about Croquet derive, however, from its first vogue in the middle of the last century. Turn over yellowing numbers of *Punch*, and you find young ladies in crinolines and pork-pie hats smiting a ball on which they have placed a dainty and provocative bootee. (This ingenuous method of making stop-shots was abolished eighty years ago or more ; and so was the double-hoop, like the cross-ribs of a Norman vault, with a bell suspended in the middle. I have recently played with the featherweight little mallets and wooden balls of the period : it is like trying to carve a sirloin with a soup spoon, they are so unresponsive.) In those days there were often eight players, whereas now there are only four or two. Impetuosity was more valued than tactical acumen, and ambition was satisfied not by a triple peel but by banging the enemy's ball into a clump of rhododendrons.

If we can believe *Punch*, the game was in especial favour with the younger and more flirtatious members of the clergy ; and some confirmation of this can be found in the novels of Charlotte M. Yonge. Her works are seldom known nowadays except to those who were brought up on them in old-fashioned homes ; but I have heard several distinguished novelists speak of her technique with bated breath. She is subtle and penetrating in the portrayal of character ; the dialogue is lively ; the intensity of emotion is morbid beyond comparison (she is a dab at death-beds). As a novelist she is not, in my opinion, inferior to Trollope, except that her subject-matter is immensely more limited. She writes chiefly about country dwellers who belong to the gentry or the professional class, and who have been influenced by the Tractarian Movement. Miss Yonge, who is extravagantly austere in her censure of everything in the least worldly or frivolous, does not condemn Croquet in itself ; but she suggests that it is alarmingly seductive. She shows it tempting both a young business-man and a curate to neglect their labours. The eldest brother in *The Pillars of the House* (my favourite among her books) forgets for once his responsibilities when he is first introduced to the game ; and in *The Clever Woman of the Family* a young wife who is something less than earnest meets her retribution, death, as a result of tripping over a hoop.

The action of these two novels is placed about the middle of the century. In England, Croquet became popular in the 'fifties. It was introduced from Ireland, where it seems to have been invented some twenty years earlier. The origin of the game is obscure, and even its name is unaccountable. The French word *croquet* means alternatively a dry biscuit, a barnacle-goose, a crosspatch or (in *patois*) a shepherd's crook. Why then should it have been chosen by the Anglo-Irish to denote their new recreation ? Croquet did not develop into a skilled affair of tactics and tournaments till the late 'sixties. The All England Croquet Club was founded at Wimbledon in 1868. Nine years later the purpose of the club was enlarged to include the new game, Lawn-Tennis, which soon cuckooed Croquet out of its nest, and in due course made the Wimbledon Club world famous.

About 1883 Croquet almost disappeared as an organized game.

(I take these facts from a recent and commendable book *Croquet Today*, by Maurice B. Reckitt, which is, however, more concerned with practical advice than with history.) In 1894 there was a revival, and Croquet continued to gain popularity until the war of 1914. Since then there have been only two important changes in the game : the two pegs at the end of the court have been replaced by one at its centre ; and as a player gets ahead he has to concede a 'lift' to his opponent. (This is to prevent the player who first obtains control of the situation from winning in the next two turns.)

One distinction of Croquet is that there are no professional players. Experts can coach out of kindness or missionary enthusiasm but not for a fee. The handicapping system is extremely effective, based upon bisques, that is to say extra turns that the weaker player can take when he chooses. The differences between an expert, an average performer and a duffer are no less marked than at Lawn-tennis or Bridge. Played by a champion with flawless precision the game looks delusively easy —but only to those who have not tried it. Watching Mr E. P. Cotter, for instance, I have felt it was useless for me ever again to touch a mallet.

THE LAST CROQUET GAME OF THE SEASON *by Arthur Hopkins*, 1895

From LONDON AT PLAY *by Gustave Doré*

Croquet is played today with undiminished zest and greater skill than ever before at Roehampton, Hurlingham and a certain number of clubs in the country. But private lawns are rare. They require careful upkeep and are four times as large as Lawn-Tennis courts. (Great pleasure can be obtained, however, from a court of less than regulation size.) Played at a club, the game costs less than Golf or

Lawn-Tennis : mallets and balls last for years. The great disadvantage of Croquet is that the enjoyment depends so much upon the weather. It is not played during the winter months. (If it returns to fashion, as I hope it may, perhaps *en tout cas* courts could be made with something like *crêpe* rubber ?) Nor does summer in England provide regularly the proper climate for Croquet. Enthusiasts will play on cold and even wet days, but often one must wait for a quarter of an hour while another player makes a long break ; and this is dreary unless the sun is shining and the wind is absent. I cannot pretend that even in the best weather it is very amusing to watch one's opponent proceed through twelve hoops by a method that has become a formula. Impatient characters complain that Croquet can be as bad as fishing, and I have sometimes longed for a book to read.

When the English summer is its too usual sad self, there is a great deal to be said for Golf-Croquet, because of its brisk pace. The regular game, as played in tournaments, seems to me dull ; but change the rules, make it necessary to run both balls instead of only one through the hoop in order to score the point, and the tactical interest becomes prodigiously more acute. Golf-Croquet loses little when it is played on a court much smaller than the regulation size, and irregularities in the surface are far less exasperating than at proper Croquet. The game can be very delightful even on a lawn with a slope ; and I have enjoyed playing on one court with a fountain in its middle that provides an unconventional hazard. Though skill always dominates, less skill is required, because some of the most difficult strokes never have to be attempted.

Croquet, real Croquet, becomes an Elysian game when the conditions are ideal. The day must be cloudless and windless ; there will be congenial players with whom to chat ; ideally there should be roses on one side of the court, a herbaceous border on another ; and then a view over a park towards a lake with swans ; and a clump of cedars at hand, with layers of green shade under which are spread drinks and strawberries. The sun sinks, the game continues till darkness gently veils the lawn, and rather than leave the struggle undecided one fetches an electric torch with which to guide one's partner to victory at the peg.

THE AERIAL ADVENTURERS

by C. H. GIBBS-SMITH

IT WAS PERHAPS appropriate that the first air pilots of the world were men of the eighteenth century, and that in the Age of Reason it should have been two of Voltaire's countrymen who made the first aerial voyage of all time, in 1783. This followed close upon a gala trial ascent put on at Versailles before the King and his court, when a sheep, a cock and a duck were sent up in a basket, all to land safely except for an injured wing—the cock's—caused by a vigorous kick from the sheep.

The new vehicle born to science was of course the hot air balloon, and there was a certain added charm in the fact that its creators—the brothers Montgolfier of Annonay, near Lyons—had developed their invention into a man-carrying balloon without knowing what lifted it. For their fuel was straw and wool, and they thought the noxious smoke given off was a new and magical gas, until the scientists of Paris took a look at the business and came to the right conclusion about the heated air. But the learned gentlemen of Europe had little to be proud of in the sphere of balloons until the brilliant Professor Charles designed the hydrogen balloon in that same year 1783 ; for anyone could have constructed a successful hot-air balloon from the earliest times at which silk or linen fabrics had been woven. But nobody, until the half-forgotten Father Gusmao in 1709—whose work was soon submerged —and the shrewd French paper-makers had drawn the necessary dramatic parallel from watching scraps of burnt-out debris go sailing into the air above a bonfire.

From a small balloon released before an awe-struck crowd at Annonay in 1782, the brothers had gone on to make bigger and brighter balloons until the great day came when they were ready to set one of their monsters loose in Paris with human pilots aboard, after careful tests with it tethered to the ground, as well as the animal voyage already mentioned. Ballonophiles are careful to record the great flight as the first *aerial voyage*—a free unfettered flight—because, strictly speaking, the tethered ascents were flights, but not proper ones.

The 21st day of November 1783 inaugurated the air age, one hundred and twenty years before the Wright brothers flew over the lonely sands of Kitty Hawk, North Carolina. On that afternoon the delightful gardens of the Château de la Muette in the Bois de Boulogne were packed with excited Parisians; and on a large raised platform before them rose the great swaying form of the Montgolfiers' finest creation. It was 74 feet high, and magnificently decorated in blue and gold with fleurs-de-lis, the signs of the zodiac, the Royal cipher, shining suns and other gay motifs. Round the neck of the balloon was fixed a wicker gallery for the aeronauts, and slung in the neck itself was a brazier with burning straw and wool to keep up the supply of hot air once the machine was flying. The great linen envelope, lined with paper, was first suspended limp between two poles and a fire lit beneath a hole in the platform to inflate the envelope ready for take-off.

The crowd was already impatient, as the balloon had been damaged two hours before during a preliminary captive test. But all was now repaired and ready, and her pilot, the physician Pilâtre de Rozier, with his noble passenger, the Marquis d'Arlandes, went aboard. The King had previously ruled that only criminals should be sent up in these new sky vehicles, but had rescinded his unpopular decision when it was pointed out to him that the honour of France was at stake.

'The aerostat,' says a contemporary account, 'left the ground at 54 minutes past one o'clock, passed safely over some high trees, and ascended calmly and majestically into the atmosphere.' At an altitude of 280 feet the aeronauts took off their elegant hats and waved to the multitude—the approved gesture of aeronauts to show they were alive —and went bravely on their way. They crossed the Seine and flew steadily over Paris, passing near the Invalides and the École Militaire; but on approaching Saint-Sulpice they had to stoke the brazier to gain enough lift to clear some houses. After a change of wind direction they flew south, and, twenty-five minutes after their take-off, they landed gently in a field near the Gobelins, having then travelled five and a half miles from their starting point.

By great good fortune the Marquis' transcript of the conversation held on this famous flight has come down to us—the first piece of aerial reporting—and some of the passages convey a curious charm, especially when it is remembered that the men had to stand on opposite sides of the gallery and were out of sight of one another:

'At this time, Mr. Pilâtre said, *You do nothing, and we shall not mount.*

Pardon me, I replied. I threw a truss of straw upon the fire.' The Marquis seems to have done most of the work, even having to sponge out a small fire in the fabric. A few minutes later, after stoking the brazier vigorously to make the balloon rise, they felt a jolt : 'I said then, What are you doing ? Are you dancing ? *I don't stir*, said he. So much the better, replied I, it is then a new current, which I hope will push us over the river.' And so this.dignified colloquoy continued until they finally touched down.

It is hard to convey the effect of this flight upon the civilized world. 'If we consider for a moment,' wrote Cavallo, 'the sensation which these first aerial adventurers must have felt in their exalted situation, we can hardly prevent an unusual sublime idea in ourselves. Imagine a man elevated to such a height, into an immense space, by a means altogether new. . . . Reflect on the prospect, the encomiums, and the consequences ; then see if your mind remains in a state of quiet indifference.'

It is sad but interesting to relate that the first aerial crossing of the English Channel—in 1785—should have been accomplished by a French pilot and an American passenger ; or rather an American doctor who was a faithful subject of King George and retired to England rather than live under the new republic. It was he, too, who financed the historic trip, and for his pains was nearly cheated out of his place in the basket by the wicked machinations of the Frenchman.

Jean-Pierre Blanchard was an intrepid but curious character, 'a petulant little fellow, not many inches over five feet, and physically well suited for vapourish regions.' He was an ardent adventurer whose chief contribution to flying was his avidity for making 'first' ascents, which he did in various European countries—but not in France or England—and also the United States. He was therefore devoted to the idea of being first across the Channel by himself, a secret he did not confide to the honest Dr John Jeffries, who patiently looked on while the balloon was inflated on the heights by Dover Castle during that cold morning of January 7, 1785.

When all was ready, Blanchard declared that the balloon would lift only one, and an explosive situation was saved only by the intervention of the governor of Dover Castle, after it was revealed that Blanchard had secretly put on a lead-lined belt to make himself heavier. However, they were obliged to patch up the quarrel and went aboard about one o'clock.

Never before or since has a balloon taken up such a miscellany of odds and ends in addition to its passengers. There were two useless aerial oars and a rudder, a 'moulinet' (revolving fan)—another ingenious but useless invention—a compass and barometer, a bottle of brandy, some biscuits and apples, a book of Blanchard's, two flags, two cork life-jackets, two anchors and thirty pounds of ballast.

The view was magnificent, and Jeffries was elated by the beauty of it. But it was soon evident that something was wrong. Today we can only guess that the trouble was a combination of a leaky envelope and bad piloting by Blanchard, who could not keep the balloon at a steady elevation but allowed her to go into steep and wasteful up-and-down runs. They had soon exhausted the ballast and began pitching out the less necessary items of cargo, including the food. Then they took off the useless gadgets so beloved of Blanchard and consigned them to the sea ; 'notwithstanding all which,' wrote Jeffries, 'the balloon not rising, we cut away all the lining and ornaments, both within, and on the outside of the car, and in like manner threw them into the sea.' Still it was not enough. So over went the anchors.

Three-quarters of the way across, the situation was again becoming desperate, and except for the cork jackets—which they dared not jettison—there was nothing for it but to abandon their coats, 'M. Blanchard first throwing away his *extra coat*, with his surtout ; after which I cast away my *only coat*' (Dr. Jeffries' italics in both cases). Blanchard then appears to have all but panicked, for he not only threw away his remaining coat, but tore off his trousers and sent them overboard too—on a cold January day, be it remembered.

The result of all this activity was mercifully to start the balloon on an up-run, and they not only cleared the French coast but went too high above and beyond it ; and again the shivering aeronauts were somewhat repaid by the excellent view. But there was still trouble ahead, because a balloon will soon go into a down-run which, if not checked by throwing ballast, will become faster and faster : and they had no ballast left. The balloon was descending rapidly over the beautiful forest of Guînes, some twelve miles inland from Calais, and as they swept down over the trees Dr. Jeffries records that they had even to resort to a 'curious' expedient—the containers for the fluid being bladders—to lighten the balloon by even a fraction before she went crashing through the tree tops and they managed to grasp some branches and bring her to a standstill.

The two men were welcomed in Calais like conquering heroes, and Blanchard was given a Royal pension of fifty pounds. As a more permanent reminder of this epic flight a picturesque monument was erected in the forest to mark the exact spot of their landing.

One of the more picturesque episodes of ballooning history was the first aerial journey made by an Englishwoman, the plumply handsome actress, Mrs Letitia Ann Sage, on June 29, 1785. The whole business had at first proved nearly a fiasco, and then might well have ended in tragedy. For when the flight was finally made, her only companion was a Mr George Biggin, and neither of them had ever been in a balloon before. The pilot chivalrously stayed behind so as not to disappoint his passengers, because his balloon refused to lift the three of them !

Vincent Lunardi, secretary to the Neapolitan ambassador in London, had been the first to make an aerial voyage in England, on September 15, 1784, from the Artillery Grounds at Moorfields, to Ware in Hertfordshire. He immediately became the hero of the day, and was given—amongst other marks of esteem—an honorary commission in the Honourable Artillery Company.

In 1785 he had a second balloon constructed, and as a graceful tribute to this country, the envelope was hugely decorated with the

---

By courtesy of the present owners, the P. & O., we show on the opposite page a unique document of ballooning history, a reproduction in colour, published here for the first time, of the finest aeronautical picture of the eighteenth century, which commemorates the Biggin–Sage voyage to Harrow. This charming 'conversation piece' was thought to have been lost, and historians will be relieved to know that it has survived and is in safe and appreciative hands. It is the original painting by J. F. Rigaud, from which the widely known Bartolozzi engraving (in two states) was made and published in 1785. Not the least of its interest lies in the pictorial inaccuracy ; for, as we have seen, Lunardi did not go up with the couple. The artist must have made portrait sketches of the three before or after the first failure to ascend together (on 13 May, 1785) and then portrayed them in the situation in which they should have been, and hoped to be later. As the engraving was published in London on June 25 (i.e., before the successful Biggin–Sage flight on June 29) the original picture, or at least a detailed sketch, must have been completed some time previously. Lunardi is here seen resplendent in his Honourable Artillery Company uniform, with Mrs Sage gracefully seated, and Biggin checking the barometer which the lady afterwards broke. The elaborate bulk of the heavy 'drapes' is well shown, together with an imaginary cannon (lower right) which, if it had been carried in reality, would have kept the balloon firmly on the ground.

THE THREE FAVOURITE AERIAL TRAVELLERS
George Biggin, Mrs Sage, Vincent Lunardi
Oil painting on copper, 1785, by J. F. Rigaud
By Courtesy of the P. & O.
(*See footnote opposite*)

Expérience de la Machine Aërostatique de M. Mongolfier au Chât. de la Muette, le 21 9bre 1783.

The first aerial crossing of the English Channel, by Blanchard and Jeffries, 1785. *Above :* a Bowles & Carver print of the departure from Dover Castle. *Below :* the arrival between Calais and Boulogne, drawn by Desrais and engraved by Bonvalet.

Above : The Ascent
of George Biggin
and Mrs Sage in
Lunardi's balloon,
June 29, 1785.
Oil painting by
Julius Caesar
Ibbetson.
*By courtesy of
Arthur Kauffman, Esq.*

Below : An ascent
by James Graham
at Lord's Cricket
Ground, Marylebone
Sept. 12, 1837.
Watercolour drawing
by Robert Bremmel
Schnebbelie.
British Museum

Union Jack and the Royal Arms of King George III. Lunardi had offered to take his friends George Biggin and Mrs Sage for a trip, but when it came to the appointed day (May 13), the balloon would not lift the three of them and Lunardi went up on his own. Mrs Sage said later that this first aerostatic fiasco brought upon poor Lunardi 'many illiberal reflections.' No one today knows why the balloon was so inefficient, but it was probably due to a combination of leaky envelope, insufficient inflation, and the heavy 'drapes' and decorations on the basket. It is also necessary, although ungallant, to relate that Mrs Sage weighed, on her own admission, fourteen stone.

However, Lunardi was determined to fulfil his promise, and all was set for another ascent from St George's Fields on June 29, although some of the actress's friends tried to dissuade her from venturing into the air. Inflation of the balloon had started at nine in the morning, and shortly after one o'clock Lunardi thought that his fine balloon contained enough hydrogen to lift the three of them, if not more. Mrs Sage, who had meanwhile been sitting in her carriage, was escorted to the balloon and helped into the 'car'—as the basket was then called. But there was already quite a company on board, including a Colonel Hastings and another lady whose name has not survived.

Lunardi tested the lift of the balloon and found he had too much weight on board to rise. So out went the unknown lady. Then he tried again and the freight was still too heavy. This time Lunardi himself stepped out. But even now the balloon would not lift its cargo. Whereupon Colonel Hastings 'very reluctantly quitted the gallery, for he appeared to have set his whole soul upon the voyage.'

It apparently never occurred to Lunardi to strip off some of the heavy and useless impedimenta which probably weighed as much as a man; so the balloon was released at 1.25, with its two inexperienced passengers. Mrs Sage appeared a little frightened at first, but 'collecting herself, she bid adieu to her earthly friends, and mounted on a pinnacle of height which no woman had ever before visited' —an understandable but untruthful excess of journalistic enthusiasm, for Madame Thible, of Lyons, had been the first female aerial voyager the year before, and a Mademoiselle Simonet had gone up with Blanchard in England only a month before. But Mrs Sage won the proper distinction of being the first Englishwoman to fly.

Up went the elaborately decorated balloon—nearly colliding with Astley's Amphitheatre—to the cheers of a crowd estimated at 150,000.

The voyage was decorous and comparatively uneventful, except that Mrs Sage knelt on the height-recording barometer by accident and broke it. But they were both entranced by the scenery, and they ate a meal of ham, chicken and Florentine wine.

Just before half-past two they were in a down-run, and finally decided to land : so out went the anchor, the ballast, and the remains of the food, and soon the balloon was dragging its anchor across the fields. After one unfortunate man—trying to be helpful—had been knocked over by the car, a number of people managed to catch and hold it, and the famous flight was at an end. Mrs Sage had meanwhile hurt her foot—it is not clear how—and was glad enough to climb out ; but Biggin wanted to take on more ballast and go up again. But he gave up the idea in face of the angry owner of the field, who said his property had been damaged, and because of the lack of ballast.

They found they had landed near Harrow-on-the-Hill, some thirteen miles from their starting point, and were delighted to see the celebrated headmaster of Harrow, Dr Drury, advancing towards them like a general at the head of his pupils. The Harrow boys presumably kept the angry farmer at bay, casting admiring glances at Mrs Sage's *embonpoint*, and helped to dismantle the balloon. Next on the scene came a Mr and Mrs Wilson, of Henwell Green, who took the limping and grateful Mrs Sage to their house nearby, while Biggin went off up the hill with the Headmaster for a well-earned bottle of port.

The two aerial travellers were united at Harrow School around ten o'clock that evening—Biggin having sent a carriage to collect Mrs Sage—and the pair set out on their homeward journey soon after, seen off by the cheering Harrovians. For the sake of the record, and on the authority of Mrs Sage herself in her 'Letter addressed to a Female Friend,' we should note that the lady reached her house, No. 10, Charles Street, Covent Garden, about midnight and stayed in bed next day nursing the mysteriously injured foot.

Ballooning ceased to be a craze at the end of the eighteenth century, and settled down to more than a century of service to sport, entertainment and science. The balloonists acquired names and fame rather like footballers and cricketers today, and the flights of Coxwell, Green, the Grahams, the Spencer family, and many more, added something to the total of human knowledge and a great deal to the annals of adventure before the brief renaissance of ballooning as a society sport in the Edwardian decade, and its lamented eclipse in our own day.

THE *SATURDAY BOOK* STORIES

MARIO ON THE BEACH

by LOUIS GOLDING

THE GYLLIANS run a small business in the Midlands. They never have been prosperous, and when they married and planned their family, the idea was to keep it down to two. In course of time a boy and girl appeared on the scene ; then, to their chagrin, little Bobbie arrived, too. He was an 'unwanted' child, as they say, and what is more it was found there was something wrong with the child's heart. The doctors said he would always be delicate.

The consequence was that the parents developed an outsize guilt complex regarding little Bobbie. In the effort to prevent little Bobbie guessing he hadn't been wanted they leaned over backwards till they almost broke in two. Also they got it into their heads that his unwantedness somehow accounted for his heart condition. They felt they had to make up a terrible lot to him. In other words, they spoiled him outrageously. I don't think in all my life I have come across a more spoiled child than little Bobbie Gyllian. If he was thwarted in the least degree, he would clench his little fists, beat a wild tattoo with his feet, and his screwed-up face would go a dirty grey. The parents were certain the discoloration was partly due to the heart condition, and he soon got wise to that. He had only to point a finger to get everything he wanted. He led his parents a fine dance.

When I met the Gyllian family on the Lido that summer, they only had little Bobbie with them. The elder boy and girl had been farmed out with an aunt somewhere. Suffolk was good enough for *them*. The friends I had gone out with had left some days earlier, so I found myself on the beach with the Gyllians nearly every day. It was only the Bagni Municipali we went to, not one of the smarter beaches, and that was expensive enough for us, with our exiguous allowances and our desiccated pounds. I must say that little Bobbie didn't add to the gaiety of nations for me, the way he ran around hooting like an engine, stealing little boys' toys, tweaking little girls' hair, and altogether making a nuisance of himself. And all the time his parents looked on, or rather looked away, with a slightly glazed expression. There was nothing they could do about it, as they well knew, without provoking a storm of rage, and probably a heart attack.

The Mario episode took place on a Sunday afternoon, when the beach was more than usually crowded with young people from the Giudecca and the Fondamento Nuovo and other working-class parts of Venice. Soon after our little group settled down for the afternoon —if you could ever call it settling down with little Bobbie in the offing—a dozen lads, for the most part between sixteen and nineteen years old, arrived whooping on the scene in their bathing-slips, to play football. In a minute or two, by that process of accretion which functions among boys everywhere, whether on a beach, on a village green, or in a back alley, wherever there is a ball to be kicked around, the dozen boys had become sixteen or eighteen and had divided into two teams. A moment later the goal-posts, consisting of folded jackets, had been set up, and the boys were off. They were playing barefoot with a big rubber ball, one hemisphere scarlet, the other bright blue. It was a pleasant sight, the scampering lithe young bodies, brown as hazel nuts on the brown honey sands, making a mobile frieze that changed its composition from moment to moment against the background of dream-blue sky and stone-blue sea.

[124]

I don't know how soon I became aware of the youth named Mario, though he had doubtless come on to the beach along with the others, and had been sitting on the edge of the excitement, applauding and exhorting the players. I think I first heard the name before I identified the owner. 'Mario! Mario!' cried one of the youths in the forward line. *'Guardi!* Look!' I, too, obeyed the summons, and saw a motionless lad, one arm upstretched, the other extended behind him, the body poised on tip-toe. I think the fellow may have been a muscle-man, a member of one of those clubs where young men lift tremendous weights, and stand attitudinizing in front of large mirrors, in poses they have studied from books of classical statuary.

The whole game froze where the players stood, the goal-men before their goal-mouths, the backs protecting them. No-one moved except the young man, Mario, who had been summoned by the muscleman. He, too, was in a bathing-costume, like the others.

He moved forward swiftly on big flat feet over the yellow field, his immensely long arms swinging loose. A large camera with a black strap was slung over his shoulders. I hadn't noticed him earlier because he must have been sitting facing towards us. Had he been turned in profile, or with his back turned, it would have been quite impossible not to notice him. For he was a hunchback.

The thing on his back was a huge amorphous chunk like a stuffed sack gone askew. I can't remember that I had ever seen a hunchback stripped before, on a beach, or in a Turkish bath, or any place where such a spectacle is likely to present itself. I would not like to refine too minutely on the nature of my first reaction. Probably it was disgust; if it was, I am ashamed of it. But there certainly was pity, too, and anger—anger because of the lad's hideous bad luck. But the thing I want to bring out at once is that almost instantaneously another element in the situation thrust the hump into the background of my mind. It was the lad's face, or rather its expression. It was not a handsome face, like that of several of his mates, who might have stepped straight out of one of the canvases at the Accademia across the lagoon. Indeed I can't help surmising whether both the physical and psychological drag on a hunchback's body must always prevent the face from having beauty, at least of the familiar sort.

But the *expression* on Mario's face was something so beautiful it tugged at the heart-strings. There, of course, pain in the expression both round the eyes and in the corners of the mouth; I should imagine that in a greater or lesser degree you will always find pain in a hunchback's face. But in Mario's face it was pain transcended. Yes, it was a saint's face.

At last Mario, the camera over his shoulder, had reached the point he was making for. The two teams were still as statues. One of the boys had the sole of his foot on the big ball, and only that was moving, an inch this way, an inch that way, as if of its own volition. For the time being none of the boys was in the least conscious of the ball, as it might be the greyhounds on a track losing all consciousness of the electric hare. It was only Mario the boys were conscious of. They were a very ordinary lot of boys, I should say ; it is quite likely there were several bad hats among them. But as they looked at Mario, you were aware that a sweetness came out of them, evoked by the sweetness in the hunchback's face. Let me not fight shy of the word. They loved Mario, as he loved them. They looked as if they would readily die for him.

'*Ecco !*' cried Mario, getting down on one knee. '*Va bene cosi !*' He slipped the camera-strap from round his shoulders, pointed the camera at the tip-toe muscle-man, got him into focus, and clicked the shutter.

Then the frozen game thawed. A moment later the two contrary streams were thrusting, sparkling, revolving in eddies, as if the brown bodies were water. It was only where Mario withdrew to the game's perimeter that for the necessary half-minute there was a corridor of stillness.

The game continued five minutes, six minutes, longer, with Mario on one knee on the further side of it, his head supported by the palm of his right hand, facing the players and ourselves, the small English group. I don't think he had deliberately taken up that position, his hump towards the sea, with the idea of keeping it out of sight. For shortly, without being summoned, he rose to his feet again, and moved forward, without any self-consciousness as far as I could see, to kneel and take another photograph. It was as if among these lads, who seemed to dote on him, he could slough the sack of his affliction and be just a normal straight-backed boy like any other. For a few seconds as Mario advanced, once more the players paused while he clicked his shutter. Then once more the game raced forward and backward again.

So there they were, these young men enjoying themselves and making a good deal of noise, each of them in the way young footballers do yelling at the top of his voice to the boy temporarily in possession

of the ball, demanding that the ball be passed to *him*, because it was he
and none other who had the unique opportunity, who uniquely knew
what exactly to do with the ball. It was a noisy game, I say, and yet I
was aware of a curious sense of peace and well-being.

I wonder why, I asked myself suddenly, a moment after the thought
registered. Is it because it's so heart-warming to see an afflicted human
being like this Mario capable of finding himself somewhere happily
adjusted to a place in the scheme of things, to know himself not merely
tolerated by a group of friends, but loved by them ?

It's something more than that, I realized, that's making me feel so
much at ease. It's not merely the presence of Mario, but the absence of
little Bobbie. There was a feeling of real relaxation, with little Bobbie
not there. He was not far enough away for his parents to get panicky
about him. And he was alone, not with other children, so that one was
not going to hear a sudden loud howl from some wretched little creature
whom Bobbie had biffed in the stomach. I was aware that Bobbie's
parents, too, were having a real holiday, at least for ten minutes, with
Bobbie so deeply and safely preoccupied with his sand-castles. They
leaned back in their deck-chairs, their feet paddling the warm sand,
their faces tipped towards the hot sun.

So fifteen minutes and more passed, with Mario getting down on one
knee, with the boys posing for him, with Mario clicking the shutter.
He was, so to speak, the court photographer of the gang. He held the
exclusive rights. I don't know how many photographs he had taken,
before I realized that he hadn't taken any photographs at all. He was
just clicking the shutter and no more. He was not winding any spool.
There was no film to wind. I smiled ; I thought it all so charming.

Obviously the other boys knew from the beginning he wasn't
taking any photographs. Probably Mario couldn't actually afford a
film. But it didn't matter in the least to anybody. If there *had* been a
film in the camera, in this way and in this other way the negative
would have put them on record. Anyhow, if Mario wasn't able to
afford a film today, perhaps he would be able to afford a film tomorrow,
or the day after, the next time the gang went bathing to the Lido.

This was the line my thoughts were taking. I was aware that this
Mario affair had induced in me a pleasure such as I had not experienced
for a long time.

Then a voice broke in on my meditations, a shrill whirring grass-
hopper voice, the voice, as you can guess, of little Bobbie.

'What's *that*, Daddie ? What's *that* ?'

Yes, it was little Bobbie back amongst us, to prove that all happiness is transitory. I think even his parents had forgotten about him for those few minutes, but there he was, standing beside his father's deck-chair, plucking with finger and thumb at the flesh of his daddy's thigh.

'What's *that*, daddy ?' he repeated.

My heart sank. I slewed my head round, though I knew exactly what he was asking about; I knew the position he was in, the right arm thrust straight forward, the index finger pointing stiff. His father made no reply.

'I'm asking what that is, daddy !' the boy repeated ominously. 'Didn't you hear me ?' The father still said not a word. Then the tone changed. It had menace and malignance. 'I'm going to touch it ! I want to know what it's made of !'

At last Tom Gyllian found his voice.

'You mustn't !' he gasped. 'I forbid you !' I suppose it was the first time he had forbidden his child anything. By now the youths were aware that something odd was going on among the group of *forestieri* hard by. Mario had just risen from his knee after clicking the shutter of the camera. The mother had hidden her face behind her hands. The father's face was tense with apprehension. 'I forbid you !' he said again and seized little Bobbie's arm. The child tore himself free and ran off towards the footballers. His face was like a twisted lump of browny-green putty. The eyes glared like a small fiend's. The youths stared at the child incredulously, their mouths wide open. No-one put out a finger to stop him. Now at last he reached Mario. At once he started pommelling the great hump with both fists, banging away dementedly. The breath spurted from between his teeth in sharp hisses. The young men stood there and looked on, for twenty seconds, thirty seconds, stock-still. Mario said nothing; all the world's sadness was in his face.

Then the tension broke. The footballers flung themselves on the child, hurled him to the ground, and began to beat him without mercy.

A moment later we were there, the father, the mother, and I. 'Let him go !' the mother screamed hysterically. 'He's ill ! He's got a weak heart ! He'll die !' Desperately Tom and I tore at the limbs of the young men, trying to prise them away from the small boy. We might have been pulling at so many tree-trunks in a wood. No, it was not we who saved Bobbie.

'For the love of Christ, stop !' cried a voice. 'Do you hear me ?

Stop !' It was the voice of Mario. The tears were streaming down his cheeks.

In a moment or two the huddle of bodies came apart. The youths got on to their feet again, shook their heads, like dogs emerging from water and, muttering, walked off this way and that. It was Mario again who raised little Bobbie from the ground, and stroked his cheeks, and took him by the hand. It was Mario who placed him in his mother's arms.

'Take him, *signora* !' he said. 'He is going to be such a good boy now. *Un bravo ragazzo*. Is that not true, *giovanotto* ?' He was talking Italian, of course.

For some minutes the child went on sobbing. He was hurt and very frightened. Mario stood there patiently, and waited, stroking away the tears with the tips of his fingers. Not even Bobbie's mother said a word. The matter did not seem to be in her hands. At last the sobbing began to peter out.

'You will be a *bravo ragazzo* from now on ?' Mario softly insisted, staring deep into little Bobbie's eyes. '*Non é vero ? Non é vero ?*'

Somehow, it is beyond me to explain how, little Bobbie understood exactly what the words meant. He opened his eyes.

'Yes, sir,' he whispered. 'I'm going to be a good boy now.'

This happened two summers ago. And I have to report that, by and large, little Bobbie *has* been a good boy from that day to this—as good as the next little boy, anyhow. And his heart has given little cause for alarm, too. It seems there was something wrong with the diagnosis. Why it has all turned out this way I can only surmise. Perhaps it is only that the father has taken a firmer hand with the young man. I don't know. To explore the question would make of this story a pediatrician's tract, and I prefer to leave it a story. Besides, the reader might care to do his own surmising.

THE OLD TOMATO

by JOSEPHINE BLUMENFELD

THEY CALLED HIM The Old Tomato and greeted him with flags when he came and when he went. The flags were kept in the hay loft over the stables and it was always a rush getting to the loft and back to the drive in time to wave them in at the car windows when they saw him coming up the drive or leaving the front door.

'Quick, boys, yer father's on his way.' Harry, the old Scotch groom, in spite of his age and bow legs, sometimes ran ahead of Charles and James and got to the loft first. No-one was certain of how or why the flag-waving business had started ; it might have been V.E. Day or the day The Old Tomato came back from the war ; no-one remembered exactly and it didn't matter much. Only Charles and James knew it most absolutely had to be done and that they liked doing it. Other children thought it was silly but fun.

'We never do things like that to our parents,' they said scornfully, but they joined in just the same.

As for The Old Tomato, no-one could call him an enthusiastic flag-waving receiver, and unless he had Lulu in the car with him he paid them not the slightest attention, neither waved 'Helloa' nor called 'Goodbye.' But if she was there he did at least let them unpack the car and take it in turns to carry in his gun case and cartridge bags. He didn't take much notice of Her Pipship either if one came to think about it, only pushed out a puce-coloured cheek for her to kiss before disappearing into the gun-room to clean his barrels, which was pretty mingy of him really because she always seemed so pleased to see him, much more pleased than she looked when they came back from school.

But birds were his things ; they knew that because they had heard Buxton telling Mrs Buxton so in the pantry while they were lying hidden in the long grass under the window.

'It's birds all the way with 'is Lordship,' Buxton had said as he spat on the glasses to make them shine.

'Shoots 'em in the autumn ; eats 'em in the winter ; and chases 'em in the spring. There was a bird I saw 'im take up with in Cairo fit to burst the combinations off a tiger, silk stockings up as far as you go and not a fly on 'er. Them flies were a fair plague I can tell you, in and out of babies' eyes and up the turnings of yer trousers.'

Mrs Buxton sat back in her chair, the wicker one which creaked, and picked her ear with a hairpin.

'Wicked shame,' she muttered, 'and them poor little boys growing to be such a lovely age for boys.'

Charles and James emerged on hearing themselves alluded to in such soppy terms and went into the hay loft to discuss the bird question. Instead, they looked over the flags, flicked them out and straightened them, because Her Pipship had said earlier on that The Old Tomato was coming back about six. She had looked pleased and had given them sixpence.

Now they saw that the French flag was torn, ripped half-way up the middle, and the Union Jack harbouring a family of spiders. It was full of dust when they shook it, it was too big to be wieldy, they got it round their legs, tripped up, and fell on old knee scars which opened again with splinters from the wooden boards. Only the Japanese flag was in really good condition, with its charming little rising sun in one corner, but Her Pipship had forbidden them to wave it because the Japaneses had been against The Old Tomato and Scotland during the war. The Stars and Stripes had been all right until James had used it to wrap up his white rabbit when it had a cough, but now it was chewed and messed up round the stars and seemed to have lost much of its original gaiety.

They hoped Lulu would be with The Old Tomato when he came. Lulu was Wizard. She smelt of bath salts, and wore flowers on her coat. She was prettier than Her Pipship and much smaller. She laughed all the time and took their side when it was time for bed. That was probably because she was French. A boy at school said he knew a French boy who was allowed to stay up all night drinking red wine. But Mrs Buxton didn't like foreigners of any description : she said they ought to stay in their own countries, however uncomfortable they were. Charles and James thought Lulu was 'Bang On.' Once she had brought them a whole box of liqueur chocolates made into the shapes of bottles, which they had quaffed in the loft till they felt quite drunk—anyway till they thought they were drunk—and they couldn't stand up straight ; then they pushed each other down the loft ladder and giggled helplessly as they rolled about in the straw.

Lulu's husband was a French Count who lived in a château and made wine from his own vineyards. Buxton had been billeted in a château during the first world war but he didn't think anything of them at all. 'Dolled up with gold chairs and statues. Shut-up shutters, and not a flower bed you'd own to. The backyards turn your stomach,' he said.

Still, they hoped Lulu would come this evening because then The Old Tomato would be in a good mood; he might even get up a game of cricket and make Her Pipship and Lulu play as well. Lulu was awfully funny when she played, trying to run in high heels and tight skirts. She let out screams of French fright if the ball came anywhere near her ; sometimes she even ran away and hid behind the trees, then she had to be dragged back by them and The Old Tomato.

But when six o'clock came and they saw the car coming up the drive they lowered their flags to half-mast because they could see that The Old Tomato was alone and cross. His face was as purple as the thistles which grew in the glen below the garden, and he was sucking at his pipe so ferociously that clouds of smoke filled the front of the car ; but even if he were on fire they still had to wave the flags, and Charles went so far as to poke the end of the French one in at the window of the car.

But he passed them by without a nod, jumped out, left the car door open and disappeared into the house.

They didn't see him again that evening, though they waited for a long time stiff and straight in their beds in case he should come up to say 'Good night.' They could hear his voice and Her Pipship's in the room below, a drone which rose and fell in pitch and volume and seemed to go on for ever. All this was out of order because as a rule The Old Tomato hardly spoke to Her Pipship, and now because of this talking she hadn't come upstairs either. Charles didn't say anything to James and James didn't let on to Charles, but they were both aware of an emptiness, a new unease, which they had never felt before, and they only dropped off to sleep because they couldn't keep awake any longer.

In the morning the feeling was no less strange ; Her Pipship looked as though she had been crying, she blew her nose all through the porridge course and when it came to toast she stood up suddenly and said : 'Daddy will be leaving in a few minutes.'

They gulped down the rest of their breakfast and rushed off to the loft for the flags and when they got back to the house The Old Tomato was already in the hall giving Buxton instructions—who was still in his shirt-sleeves and green baize apron.

The floor was strewn with luggage, suit-cases, hold-alls, fishing rods, gun cases and the funny-shaped white cardboard box which contained the top hat he wore for weddings and race meetings. Thistle, the liver-and-white spaniel, whined round the luggage wagging her stubble tail expectantly, and suddenly The Old Tomato shouted 'Car, Thistle!' and she leapt through the open door into the front seat and sat bolt upright like Royalty, not bowing or smiling to any of them. At last everything was packed in. Buxton stood respectfully outside the door with slightly bowed head, staring at the gravel on the drive as if he had never seen it before. The Old Tomato gave a sharp glance at Her Pipship, thrust out a red cheek, let it rest for a second on her pale one, then without a sign to anyone else climbed into the driving seat beside Thistle.

Charles and James ran ahead to take up their stands by the posts and as the great car crunched over the drive and nosed its way through the gates they waved the flags with their usual enthusiasm, Britain, France, Holland and lastly the chewed Stars and Stripes. The Old Tomato's face was inscrutable, his red moustache bristling, his yellow eyes staring straight ahead ; then suddenly and to their great surprise he raised his hat as he passed them and blew the horn.

They waved and cheered the departing car. 'Good old Old Tomato,' they cried, and gave a last and final wave of each flag in order of precedence.

When the car was out of sight they dragged their flags behind them back to the house. Mrs Buxton was standing on the step. She looked solemn and grey, like a torn dishcloth.

'Put down them flags' she said, as she came towards them, and she clutched the backs of their necks with her thick red hands.

'Your mother wants you both in the morning room,' she said, and she pushed them towards the door.

Her Pipship was sitting with bent head and hands clasped on her lap on the window seat. Her face was in the shadow but she lifted her head when they came in and said, 'Sit down, boys : I want to talk to you.'

All the wrong things they had done during the last week came suddenly into their minds : Mrs Buxton's apple-pie bed, the spider in

Buxton's tooth glass, the tins of condensed milk in their house under the roof, the squirrel they had enticed into the nursery which was now being house-trained in the linen cupboard, the tadpoles in the treacle-tin on the pantry shelf, these and a multitude of other wrong things loomed large and frightening. Oddly enough it wasn't any one of them, but about The Old Tomato, and Her Pipship's voice was low and strained and difficult to follow. 'You must try to understand what I'm telling you,' she said. 'He has gone away. He often goes away, yes, I know he does, but this time it's for good, and he won't be coming back. You see, he likes someone else better than me ; and . . . '

'I know who it is, it's . . .' James stood up suddenly and was just going to say 'Lulu' when Charles gave him a kick on the shin and dragged him back on to the sofa and hissed 'Shut up' at him in his ear. But Her Pipship didn't seem to have noticed the interruption and went on in her new low voice :

'Even grown-up people change their minds sometimes and want to be married to other people more than the people they are already married to, and that's what's happened to Daddy, you see ; and so if that's what he really wants, it's better that way I think : don't you ?'

She didn't look up, but she paused, and they both together said eagerly, 'Oh, yes ! Much better !' because they had to say something. Then she got up and went towards the door. 'Buxton will take you rabbiting before lunch,' she said, and the next minute she had gone.

For a little while they stayed where they were on the sofa, staring at the carpet, the wood-basket, their own dirty fingers and the morning paper which had slipped off a table on to the floor. So The Old Tomato had scrammed. He hadn't even said good-bye.

Charles was the first to move.

'Come on,' he said, 'it's no good sitting there like a mouldy cow. Buxton will be waiting.'

But on their way to find Buxton they collected the flags and took them into the loft.

'Put them in the middle of the floor.' Charles gave the order and he suddenly looked stern and much older than he was.

'Criss-cross them one on top of the other. Now shove this paper underneath and when I strike the match stand back or you'll burn your wig. After that follow my orders.'

James's hand shook as he bundled the newspaper into a ball and pushed it under the heap of flags. The sticks were dry and the cloth caught at once. Soon the flames rose high and James followed Charles's orders when he called, 'One, Two, Three. Jump on them. Stamp on them. Put them out.'

Frightened by the flames, but urged on by their purpose, they stamped and jumped on the burning flags and waved their arms about their heads like native warriors round a camp fire. Their cheeks burned from the heat of the flames, they screwed their eyelids against the flying sparks and as the intensity of the heat grew so they stamped with renewed vigour, chanting in their high-pitched schoolboy voices in time to their war dance : 'Down with him. Down with him. Down with The Old Tomato.'

THE COOL OF THE EVENING

by ANNA McMULLEN

HE BOYS, who had been flinging off their clothes by the rocks on the far side of the cove, scampered down the hot sand to the sea. Some waded in ; some ran in, knees high ; others threw themselves in. Then each one, prompted by parental orders, wet his head in his own manner. The shining calm of the water was broken. Laughing, gasping, they slipped and clutched ; dived at each others' legs, swam, floated and splashed.

A tall, thin boy came up from a duck-dive and pushed the dripping hair off his forehead with both hands. 'Where is Liz ?' he said.

'Liz ! Liz !' they cried, happy to have a reason for making a noise. 'Are you coming, Liz ?' they shouted, cupping their mouths with wet hands. Then quickly they turned to the water again.

To the girl, undressing behind the big boulder, the shouts and splashings sounded hollow, as though she stood in a cave. And indeed, under the shadow of the boulder it seemed as cool and dim as in a cave. The sand was damp, and when she pressed with bare toes moisture welled up between them.

'Coming,' she called, without much conviction, knowing that she had not been heard above the clamour.

She undressed slowly, first throwing her few clothes on to a rock, and then, as an afterthought, retrieving them and hanging them carefully on a knob of the boulder. When she was naked she stood pressing her toes down into the sand. She rubbed her forearm across her lips, sniffing. It had the satisfactory scorched smell of tanned skin. Idly she pushed at a limpet, trying to detach it with her finger-nail.

'Liz is either dreamy or noisy, these days,' she had heard her mother sigh to Aunt Ashford, the pair of them now sitting together on a rug, her mother's hat nodding as they talked and knitted. 'It's her age,' her aunt had replied, comfortably.

The limpet stuck as tightly as the barnacles. Liz poked it impatiently. She looked down at her body. It had certainly changed since last summer. This, she supposed resentfully, must be the reason why these holidays seemed different. Uncertainty and bewilderment had clouded her pleasure since that day when, chattering round the table in the old nursery, she and the boys had planned an early morning trawling expedition in old Sam's smack.

'I don't think you can go, Liz,' her mother had said, briefly, and in answer to Liz's furious enquiry, had replied, 'Six hours in the smack is a long time. . . . No sanitation,' she added vaguely, her voice trailing off. 'It is no longer quite suitable.'

Liz pulled on her bathing dress. It felt tight across her chest. Picking up her towel, she ran, long legs flashing furiously, down to the edge of the sea, and flung herself in.

'Your bathing cap, Liz !' her mother wailed.

Liz swam violently, and tossed the wet hair out of her eyes. 'Girls *have* to wear bathing caps,' mocked a small boy.

'They do *not*,' said Liz. 'Damn caps !' she added vehemently, glancing sideways at the tall boy. 'Race you, Tom ?'

Her mother laid down her knitting with a sigh, and started to unpack a tea basket on to a white cloth. 'She has always wanted to be a boy,' she said.

'It's being brought up with them,' said her sister. 'What with her brothers, and my boys, and their friends. . . . It will all be the same in a few years,' she added, flapping lazily at a wasp.

Winning the race was, in some odd way, disappointing. Liz waded over to the rocks through sea so calm she could see her shadow on the sandy bottom, and tiny fishes darting round her toes. Sitting in a warm pool, ringed round with sea anemones, their red fringes gently swaying, she put her finger into one velvet centre, and felt it close with astonishing firmness. She pushed off from the rocks and swam out as quietly as possible, hoping not to be noticed. She turned over and floated. There is no-one, nothing, she said to herself. I am the sea, the blue sky, the white gull over the green cliff. This is happiness.

'Come out now, Liz,' called her mother.

'Tea, Liz, tea !' shouted the boys, running from the rocks, shaggily dressed, wringing out bathing drawers and trying to comb tangled hair.

Pushing and scrambling, scuffling sand on to the cloth, they all settled down, brown legs crossed, and began to eat enormously.

'Hi, Liz, a jam puff for your phiz !' her brother rhymed, pushing a plate with sandy toes.

'No, Robert ! Not with your feet !' said his mother, helplessly.

'I can't eat a puff, I've had quite enough !' said Liz, pushing it back. Then they all started rhyming, and rolled, doubled up in the sand, choking with laughter until the tears ran down their faces.

*　　*　　*　　*　　*

Tom had just hit the ball to Liz, who, dropping it, had thrown it back rather viciously, when the motor boat thumped round the headland, now turning black against a pinkish-green sky. They pulled on wet, gritty gym shoes, gathered up belongings, and carried them down to the boat, which had glided quietly on to the beach.

'Where is the second boat ?' they asked the old man.

He looked concerned.

He hadn't known there was to be one. There must have been some mistake. It appeared there would be no second boat.

There was a moment of mingled consternation and delight. 'Hooray !' cried the little boys. 'Can we camp here all night ?'

'Quietly,' said Aunt Ashford—Liz's mother was looking distraught—'We must think.'

They all thought, the children noisily. It was arranged that as many as the boat would hold should go by sea, taking the picnic paraphernalia. The rest would have to climb the cliff and walk over the fields to the ferry, where Uncle Ashford, warned by the boat party, would meet them with the dinghy and row them home across the river. Liz's mother was to go in the boat. 'And you, and you and you,' said Aunt Ashford, prodding various small boys, who screamed with rage and disappointment. 'You can walk with me, Tom,' she said to her son, 'And you, too, Robert. What about Liz ?'

'Of course I shall walk,' said Liz, tensely, and threw her bathing things into the boat.

'Oh, no !' shouted the little boys, dancing round her. 'You are a girl, girls are women, and women *always* take to the boats.'

'Stop splashing,' said Aunt Ashford. Glancing briefly at Liz, she added, 'Good, I was hoping you would walk with me.'

Having helped to push the motor boat off, the little group on the beach, possessed by a feeling of isolation, stood watching as it thudded out to sea, crowded with waving, shouting figures. As it rounded the headland, Aunt Ashford sketched a half gesture. It might have been a farewell, or an imaginary brushing away of whatever anxiety she felt for Liz's mother, alone and unsupported, in charge of that wild crew. It seemed, then, unnaturally quiet. But soon the tiny

[138]

waves, which had been toppling languidly onto the beach, were swollen by the wash from the boat, and broke with a short, sharp crash, almost reaching their feet before disappearing abruptly into the shingle. When the water was quiet again, they turned their backs on the sea.

The cliff, although high, was not steep. The few yards of red sandstone at the bottom soon merged into a green tangle of grass, bracken and brambles. There were no distinct paths, though an occasional rabbit run showed red through the green. Liz felt excited and energetic. She took the first few yards at a run, and was inclined to chatter.

'You'd better take it easy, Liz,' said her aunt, breathlessly. She had found the first few steep yards a little trying, and did not really appreciate Robert's efforts to push her up from behind. Indeed, all of them soon found it necessary to retire into their own private struggles with the brambles and the tall bracken, their own search for rabbit paths to make the way easier. Robert followed his aunt, who levered herself along with her walking stick. Tom climbed ahead of his mother, sometimes holding back a trailing bramble shoot for her, and occasionally glancing up at Liz who, although quiet now, still fought her way ahead of them, finding her own paths. Now and then they all stopped for a rest, breathing in the smell of bruised bracken, and looking up to the green cliff-edge above them, which cut through a clear turquoise sky.

Reaching at last the slightly overhung ledge at the top, where a post, black against the sky, stood like a cliff-top sentinel, Liz turned and looked back. The sea seemed a long away below her, iridescent like the inside of an oyster shell, dark in the corners of the cove. The toiling figures were only just below her. She felt a surge of affection for her aunt's solid figure, a feeling which embraced also Tom, and his dear solicitude for them all. When her aunt was near enough, Liz stretched out a hand to her. Always fearful of hurting by rejection, Aunt Ashford took it, although she would have preferred to continue using her stick. Robert was already over the top, having heaved himself up by the post. Tom did the same, and helped his mother over. Then he held out a hand to Liz. She hesitated, and then, saying, 'Thanks, Tom, I can manage,' swung herself up.

But the post had stood too much. It snapped through instantaneously, with a sharp crack, and Liz slithered down several feet into a blackberry bush.

Aunt Ashford calmly restrained Robert from rushing over the edge again. Liz, having painfully disentangled herself, and holding her eyes wide open so that the tears should not brim over, took Tom's hand, and was hauled over the edge.

Still breathing hard, but laughing now, they rested on the cliff top and examined Liz's scratches, exclaiming at each one. Dabbing at the blood, they tied Tom's handkerchief round the worst one on her leg. 'They don't really hurt,' Liz said, wincing.

'They will, when Mum puts iodine on,' said Robert, who was a little jealous of such honourable wounds.

'Come now,' said Aunt Ashford. 'Put on your sweaters. We must get along.'

They walked through fields of stubble, which felt knobbly through their gym shoes, and over pastures already wet with dew. Aunt Ashford, with Robert chattering beside her, walked ahead. Liz followed quietly with Tom. The air was cool now, and sweet with country smells released by the damp air of dusk. 'This is "the cool of the evening,"' Liz said to herself.

'You were very brave, Liz,' said Tom, hesitantly.

'I was *nearly* crying,' she exclaimed, in a sudden burst of candour.

'Sometimes it is brave to cry,' he answered.

Liz could not bother to ask him what he meant, or to question this statement which was so contrary to their code. She felt content, and weariness gave her an unusual detachment. She was hardly aware of her smarting legs. Movement seemed so easy and effortless, she felt she might be floating on the mist that lay like milky water in the hollows. Had she been fully aware that Tom was helping her over the stiles she would have refused his help angrily.

But when they left the country, entered the streets of the little town, and came down to the jetty, the sudden brightness shocked Liz into conscious delight. The children had not often been out at this hour. All along the quay, and over the river, dark and oily, were scattered red, green and white lights. The big ferry-boat was half-way across; the water tumbled glistening off its paddles; all its portholes were reflected in the water like orange moons. On the opposite shore lighted windows winked like stars.

The dinghy was at the bottom of the green, slimy steps, knocking gently against the wall. Uncle Ashford was waiting in it, stifling a yawn and looking amused. He told them quite firmly where to sit.

While rowing competently across the river he listened patiently to Robert's highly coloured account of the day. He had already received other equally imaginative versions from the motor-boat party.

Liz sat dreamily in the stern, trailing her hand in the water, which was faintly phosphorescent. When Tom said, 'Your hair looks quite white in the moonlight,' she only smiled vaguely, unaware of Robert's startled stare.

Once up the steps and on to the quay the other side, their little party was noisily welcomed with exclamations and enquiries, special dispensation having been given for the other children to stay up and meet them. Liz's mother, hovering anxiously in the background, wearing a long grey coat that made her look a little like a bat, greeted her sister with thankfulness, and gave up all attempts to control the gathering, which laughed, chattered, danced and pranced, looking like elves or demons—Aunt Ashford could not decide which—in the pools of light on the quay. 'Quick march, and home to bed,' she said, firmly, and led the way with her husband, never doubting that the excited children would follow her, which they did.

As they passed out of the lights into the darkness of the narrow street that led uphill to home, Tom said, 'What about some early morning fishing in Captain's Creek tomorrow, Liz, if your scratches aren't too sore?'

Liz felt quite unaccountably happy. She drew herself up, and the tightness of her cotton frock across her chest gave her great satisfaction. 'I'm *so* sorry, Tom,' she said seriously, 'I should have liked to. But it is no longer quite suitable.'

The Saturday Book

SPECIMENS
OF ART
& NATURE

MODELS AND MUSES

by JAMES LAVER

A GENERATION AGO it was the fashion to declare that we should not look for any meaning in a picture. We should be content with its 'significant form.' An artist was praised for painting his mother as if she had been a piece of cheese. But the human mind is strangely recalcitrant to such theories. It persists in taking an interest in the 'subject' of a picture, and it is surely possible to do this without falling into the error of other theorists like Tolstoy who persuaded himself that any picture of a life-boat was necessarily good. The truth is that although there have been thousands of anecdotists whose works hardly come into the category of art at all, yet some of the very greatest painters have put so much 'subject' into their works that we are still trying to plumb their meaning. Titian is an obvious example. His 'Sacred and Profane Love' still awaits its complete explanation.

Artists have had many subjects and, from the period of the Italian Renaissance, one of their favourite subjects has been Woman. They have painted her in her own character, so to speak, just as she looked in life, princess or maid-servant, professional model or their own wife. Or they have glorified her as saint—or goddess. Often the same woman has served for both, and the artist has painted her in either capacity with the same professional competence.

Writers tend to over-dramatize, or sentimentalize, such matters. The French writer Arsène Houssaye told a touching story of Titian's 'Violante.' She was the daughter, he said, of the older painter Palma Vecchio and had posed for him as the Madonna. Later she became the mistress of Titian and posed for him as Venus. In a moment of repentance she made her way to a church and found herself praying to the Virgin—and realized that the picture before which she knelt was her own image. Unfortunately, the dates do not fit—and Palma Vecchio never had a daughter.

Yet it is impossible not to take an interest in the women great artists have painted, impossible not to wonder who they were and to wish to know more about them. Was Botticelli's 'Venus' really inspired by Simonetta Vespucci ? Perhaps the most we can do is to say, with Professor Yashiro : 'Simonetta symbolized the eternal feminine ideal, a person of dreams, half spiritual ; and as Dante had his Beatrice, Petrarch his Laura, so too perhaps Botticelli had his Simonetta.'

Titian's sitters are, as we have seen, equally elusive, but we are on firmer ground with Rubens and Rembrandt, and we know a good deal about the wives and other women who posed for Boucher and Fragonard.

The relationship between artist and model was not always exempt from sorrow or even from tragedy. Greuze's model for some of his most famous pictures was a beautiful girl known to all the Latin Quarter as 'La belle Babuti.' She offered in her own person that curious blend of the virginal and the voluptuous which is the hallmark of so many of his canvases. He married her and by her extravagance and her unfaithfulness she brought him to ruin.

A French painter of the next generation, Prudhon, was made miserable by a termagant wife. The only happiness he knew was when Constance Mayer, who had been a pupil of Greuze, began to take lessons from him. She became his mistress and model as well as his pupil, took over the care of his children, and made him the only real home he had ever known. He painted of her some exquisite portraits, but her suicide brought the idyll to a close.

Rosetti's tragic relations with Elizabeth Siddall are a part of art history. When she was a shop-girl he fell in love with her fragility and melancholy. She became his model, his mistress and finally his wife. It was his remorse at her death which drove him to chloral—the 'skeleton in his cupboard' as he called it. For on the night when she took an overdose of laudanum he was away with the other type of beauty he admired, Fanny Scholl, the 'girl with the corn-gold hair.'

Whistler's 'Little White Girl' came to no tragic end. She survived him, although they had long been separated at the time of his death. He painted her and etched her portrait many times. She was his companion and his inspiration in his early days in London. Models and Muses ! How grateful should we be to all these women who have provided the great artists of the world with their subject matter and their inspiration. They often gave their men their devotion as well as their beauty. They received in return the gift of immortality.

REMBRANDT *The Artist painting Saskia*   *Glasgow Art Gallery*

HEN REMBRANDT, in 1634, married Saskia van Uylenborch, she was twenty-two and he was twenty-seven. She posed for him many times, sometimes for 'straight' portraits and sometimes in character. Her modest face and shapely body made her the ideal sitter for Bathsheba or Susannah in the Bible stories. Here he shows us himself in the act of painting her. It is a pity that artists do not think of doing this more often. Saskia bore Rembrandt four children, a son and two daughters who all died in babyhood, and Titus who was born in 1641. In the following year Saskia herself died. It was a tragically short life.

TITIAN *The Venus of Urbino, Florence, Uffizi. Below: La Bella, Florence, Palazzo Pitti*

ITIAN'S WIFE, Cecilia, who had been his model since before their marriage in 1525, died in 1530. Soon afterwards another woman, of almost the same kind of opulent beauty, begins to appear in his canvases. He painted her in a glorious Renaissance gown as 'La Bella,' he painted her, partly unclothed, as the 'Girl with a fur,' and he painted her as Venus, the famous 'Venus of Urbino,' that hymn to carnal beauty which has bewitched the world ever since. According to Vasari, this painting was 'the portrait of a favourite of Duke Guidobaldo II.'

IT WAS IN 1500, soon after his return to Florence after his long service in Milan, that Leonardo painted the portrait of Mona Lisa, the wife of Francesco del Giocondo. The 'Gioconda Smile,' mysterious, even a little sad, has always been the subject of speculation. Tradition has it that it is the smile of one listening to music, for the artist is said to have had flute players in the room while he was painting the picture. Incidentally, it is supposed to be the only portrait he ever painted, but, of course, he painted women in his religious canvases and they are all, even the aged St. Anne, of the same recognisable type, and they all, or nearly all, wear the same enigmatic smile. The so-called 'Nude Gioconda' has it too. It is a puzzling picture, little more than a sketch, and some critics have denied that it is a portrait of the same lady as 'Mona Lisa.' The hair is dressed differently and is not so dark, but the pose is almost the same and the hands are painted in very similar fashion. But would the fine Florentine lady have posed for him like this? It is a mystery, like everything else connected with, perhaps, the most astonishing man that ever lived.

LEONARDO DA VINCI
Above: La Gioconda, Paris, Louvre
Below: The Nude Gioconda
Chantilly, Musée Condé

RUBENS' FIRST WIFE, the shy little Isabella Brant, who acted as a model for many of his early pictures, died in 1626 after a happy married life of sixteen years. In 1630, when he was fifty-three, Rubens married again. His new bride was the daughter of his dead wife's sister and her name was Helena Fourment. She was then sixteen, but the picture of her in her bridal dress shows her as already a fully-formed woman. If we use the term 'Rubensesque' for her particular kind of beauty it is because her husband painted her so often. She is to be seen as all three goddesses in his 'Judgment of Paris,' as if she combined in her own person the charms of Minerva, Diana and Venus. No doubt it was in an interval of posing for such compositions that she slipped on the fur garment, and so provided her husband with yet another theme for a picture.

BOUCHER *Louise O'Murphy*   *Munich, Die Bayerischen Staatsgemaeldesammlungen*

NEARLY ALL BOUCHER's early pictures were painted with his own wife as model. She was seventeen when he married her in 1733, and proved the ideal type for the piquant nymphs and goddesses with which he peopled his canvas. However, some seventeen or eighteen years later, when Fragonard was working with Boucher, Madame Boucher was not often in the studio. But there were plenty of other models, among them three sisters of Irish origin, whom the French call Morphi, or Morphile, or O'Morphi, but whose name was probably quite simply Murphy. One was a *danseuse* at the Opera, one was a professional model at the *Académie*, and the third was, when Casanova visited the studio, '*une petite souillon*' of about thirteen. In 1753, when she was sixteen, she attracted the attention of no less a person than Louis XV. He carried her off to become the first *pensionnaire* of his newly established harem in the *Parc aux Cerfs*. It is tempting to think that Boucher's picture of *La petite Morphile* was already *en train* when the gilded coach drove up to the door and carried off this new Cinderella If so it must be the last picture for which she posed, for, when she fell into disgrace three years later, she did not return to the studio. Louis, ever generous, gave her a handsome *dot*.

as well the number must run into scores. After 1791 he saw little or nothing of her. Sir William Hamilton, British envoy at Naples, fell in love with her and, later, she became his second wife. Nelson first met her in 1793 at Naples. Almost his last thought when he was dying at Trafalgar was of her.

A hint of her later *embonpoint* may perhaps be noted in the nude drawing here reproduced. Some critics have doubted if it represents Emma, but the drawing was exhibited in her lifetime at Schomberg House, Pall Mall, with her name attached to it, apparently without protest on her part.

Lady Hamilton at the Spinning Wheel

LL THE WORLD knows something of the romantic history of Emma, Lady Hamilton. Her birth was humble and she probably never learned to read and write. But in her early days her beauty of face and figure was remarkable and she was able to inspire poets, painters and heroes. When in 1782 she became acquainted with Romney she was in her early twenties. He painted her in some two dozen 'attitudes' and 'characters,' but if we include sketches and drawings

Kenwood, Iveagh Bequest

Lady Hamilton at Prayer

GEORGE ROMNEY *Lady Hamilton as the Goddess of Health. Present ownership unknown*

VELASQUEZ *Venus and Cupid* (*The Rokeby Venus*)   *London, National Gallery*

ELASQUEZ was, for the greater part of his life, a Court painter. He painted Philip IV of Spain many times, and he immortalized on canvas the King's children, touching in their combination of regal dignity and childish innocence, their little bodies imprisoned in the farthingale of the fashionable world at an age when modern children would still be playing happily in rompers. Velasquez painted every important Spanish personage of his time, as well as a number of religious pictures, but his nudes are scarce. The Counter Reformation had introduced a new prudery into Spanish life. Even the gloomy and fanatical Philip II had not hesitated to purchase Titian's mythologies, his naked gods and goddesses, to brighten the corridors of the Escorial. But this kind of painting was now frowned upon, and Velasquez had very few opportunities of painting the nude. All the more precious therefore is his famous 'Rokeby Venus.' True to his doctrine of naturalism, she is no idealized goddess but a slim Andalusian girl, of a singularly modern type, gazing at herself in a mirror. Actually, she is not gazing at herself but at the spectator, for if we seem to see *her* face, she can see ours. The picture passed through many hands until, in 1906, it was acquired by the National Gallery from the Morritt family of Rokeby Hall. It was slashed by the suffragettes, but has been so skilfully restored that only a slight scar remains.

F WE KNOW NOTHING of the girl who posed for Velasquez' 'Venus,' we are equally ignorant of the identity of Ingres' *'Odalisque.'* He painted many 'odalisques,' and almost certainly from professional models. They represent, indeed, a kind of generalized type, the Ingres idea of woman, at once languid and voluptuous, romantic and curiously modern. What he sought above all was the sinuous arabesque of limbs in an abandoned pose. He was the master of line, a line infinitely subtle and tender. A mere outline it never was, for he was able to make it express the receding planes and the interior modelling. It was once the fashion to find fault with Ingres for being too linear, for thinking always in terms of the drawing for the picture (for everyone admitted that he was a superb draughtsman) rather than of the picture itself. Certainly a painting like the famous *'Bain Turc'* is obviously composed in the studio from a multitude of sketches. But in the painting here reproduced there seems to be something more direct, more passionate, more living. Even in his extreme old age Ingres never lost sight of *la volupté de peindre.*

JEAN AUGUST DOMINIQUE INGRES *Sleeping Odalisque. London, V. & A. Museum*

FRANCISCO DE GOYA *The Duchess of Alba*   *Madrid, The Duke of Alba*

FRANCISCO DE GOYA *La Maja Desnuda*   *Madrid, Prado*

OYA was a man of enormous vitality and, one must add, of enormous self-possession. When his famous painting of 'The Balcony' was nearing completion the Duchess of Alba saw it and remarked that he seemed to have put into it 'all the loose women of Madrid.' 'No, Madam,' he replied, 'I have reserved a place for you.' And the duchess, it is said posed for him there and then. They became lovers, and gossip and fancy have busied themselves in trying to trace in his canvases both the features and the figure of the celebrated lady. He certainly painted her several times—as herself. Did he also depict her in the two famous canvases which now hang in the Prado: 'La Maja clothed' and 'La Maja nude'?

The traditional story is that Goya was engaged in painting the lady in a state of nudity and, not unnaturally, perhaps, it proved impossible to keep such a piquant piece of information secret. Her husband got wind of the affair and resolved to call upon the artist while he was actually at work on the canvas. But Goya was warned and, by a supreme feat of virtuosity, commenced another portrait (the 'Maja clothed') and when the Duke burst in he found his wife duly—if not excessively—clothed. Some modern critics have doubted if the Duchess of Alba really figures in the two paintings, but it is by no means intrinsically impossible. Enough documents exist to show the intimacy of their relations, and the Duchess, one of the most 'emancipated' women of her time, did not suffer from any excess of prudery.

AUGUSTE RENOIR *Gabrielle seated at a Stove*   *Mrs C. Walston*

HEN SPEAKING of Renoir,' says Théodore Duret, the critic who was one of the first to appreciate the Impressionists, 'one can repeat unhesitatingly that he was above all a painter of women . . . The painters who have been inclined to paint women, and who have done it with love, have generally emerged with an ideal and an attachment to women, and afterwards have stamped her with their originality. Such was Renoir's case.' His models included working girls, midinettes, girls of the middle class and occasionally a society girl. 'During the greater part of his life he kept looking for models. When he met, in the places he frequented or on his walks, a young woman whose bearing and appearance pleased him, he would enter into conversation with her and try to induce her to pose for him.' However, when, towards the end of his life, he settled at Cagnes, his choice was more restricted. Gabrielle entered his employment as a servant, and she continued to look after him even when she became his favourite and almost his

AUGUSTE RENOIR *Le Leger*   *Merion, Pennsylvania, The Barnes Foundation*

only model. She was a great help to him in his old age when he was so crippled with arthritis that he was hardly able to hold the brushes. He painted her over and over again, sometimes clothed and occupied with various duties about the house, sometimes as a nude. She became the very type of the *femme Renoir*.

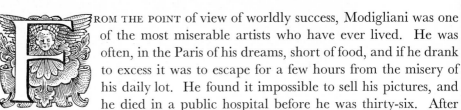

ROM THE POINT of view of worldly success, Modigliani was one of the most miserable artists who have ever lived. He was often, in the Paris of his dreams, short of food, and if he drank to excess it was to escape for a few hours from the misery of his daily lot. He found it impossible to sell his pictures, and he died in a public hospital before he was thirty-six. After his death he was recognized as a great artist, for it was at last possible to understand the deliberate deformation which he practised in his attempt to escape from the tyranny of literal interpretation. Who was the model for the drawing here reproduced? Hardly a professional, for Modigliani could never have afforded the fees. Some girl of the *Quartier Latin* perhaps, who consented to pose for a few minutes out of pity for the suffering artist?

AT HIS RECENT DEATH the whole world recognized Matisse not only as a great master but as a great master in the classical French tradition. He strove always for balance, for calm, for a final statement. Even his most apparently summary sketches are the result of long meditation. His outline has attained its astonishing simplicity at the end of a long series of preliminary studies. He loved to draw and paint the female nude, finding in the harmony of its curves the most direct expression of his ideals. The work here reproduced represents a working girl, a 'stitcher of shoe-uppers' whom he has persuaded, perhaps a little reluctantly, to pose for him. And was she pleased with her portrait when she saw it ? Probably not.

HENRI
MATISSE
*La Piqueuse de
Bottines*
Private Collection

English porcelain teapot made at Worcester, *c* 1765 (J. W. Goldsmith Collection)
Below : George III silver teapot, by Hester Bateman (John Bell Coll., Aberdeen)

THE ART OF THE TEAPOT

by GRISELDA LEWIS

N EVERY BRITISH HOME—if not, perhaps, to the same degree in American homes—the teapot has become a symbol of warmth, hospitality and friendship. It occupies the place of first importance among the household belongings and affections of the family. You can make coffee in an ordinary jug, or a pan ; you can eat fish and chips out of a newspaper ; but you can only satisfactorily perform the hallowed rite of pouring out 'a nice cup of tea' from a pot designed for the purpose.

The Chinese, who for centuries had been drinking tea, long ago evolved a suitable shape for teapots, based on the necessities of the drink. This consisted of a body in which the leaves could infuse in boiling water, a handle to hold it by that would not conduct too much heat, and a spout through which to pour the infusion without spilling it. There had to be an opening at the top through which the pot could be filled and emptied, with a lid to cover it, so that the drink could be kept hot. The body of the pot could be spherical, barrel-shaped, pear-shaped, boat-shaped, almost any shape ; but variations on the spherical form seem to have dominated all others in pottery and porcelain.

In England tea was originally drunk medicinally. It was discovered to be a pleasant and soothing drink and, though it was very expensive, it soon became a fashionable habit. Families had their portraits painted grouped round the tea table. William Hogarth painted several such 'conversation pieces,' and there is an anonymous eighteenth-century painting in the Victoria and Albert Museum, which we reproduce here on page 165, of just such another family group. By the middle of the eighteenth century tea had fallen to an average price of about seven shillings and sixpence a pound (including the duty), and tea drinking was firmly established as a national habit.

When tea was first introduced into England, somewhere about 1650, suitable pots for the brewing of the drink were imported with the chests of tea from China. These teapots were made of unglazed red earthenware, and mostly came from the town of Yi-Hsing near Shanghai. The Chinese maintained that these unglazed pots produced a better-flavoured drink than that infused in a white porcelain pot. The teapots were very small, and one was provided for each drinker.

The earliest English teapots were made of silver, but by about 1690 red earthenware teapots, in imitation of the Chinese, were being made in Staffordshire by two Dutch brothers, John and Philip Elers, who had come over from the Low Countries (where teapots were already being made) and settled in England. These Elers teapots were of a fine red earthenware, beautifully potted and decorated with simple, raised patterns in the Chinese manner. This ware was soon copied by many other potters, and a different kind of teapot was made at Nottingham, in a brown glazed stoneware with incised decorations.

During the eighteenth century a certain amount of Oriental porcelain was being imported from China by the East India Company. This, of course, was very expensive, and a real Chinese teapot could only have been within the reach of the well-to-do. In an attempt to copy this white Oriental porcelain the English potters produced white salt-glazed stoneware, which, though non-translucent and not so refined as porcelain, became deservedly popular and was made in great quantities from about 1720 to 1740. Salt-glazed ware did, in fact, continue in production throughout the eighteenth century.

A great variety of salt-glazed teapots was made in almost every imaginable shape ; camels, shells, houses, fruit and vegetables provided inspiration for the potters. The earliest salt-glazed teapots were left uncoloured, but were decorated with embossed designs, borrowed from the silver-ware of the time and retaining the crispness of outline of metal work. Later, the demand for coloured ware increased, and teapots were painted with brilliant enamel colours. On pages 168 and 169 we show a small selection of some of these teapots. These coloured teapots were generally simple in shape, and spherical ones were particularly popular. The painted decorations on them ranged from landscapes and figure subjects (sometimes with an Oriental flavour) to designs with flowers and birds, feathers, animals and even portrait medallions. Other teapots were made in the form and colouring of cauliflowers, pineapples and heads of maize.

For years the potters went on experimenting, trying to discover the secret of porcelain. A Staffordshire potter called John Astbury was the first to add calcined flints to the body of the clay he used in an attempt to whiten it still further. He made many curious teapots decorated with small stamped reliefs of trailing vines and similar subjects. The decorations were made of white clay and laid upon a coloured ground, the whole being covered with a thin lead glaze.

Thomas Whieldon, a contemporary of Astbury, made experiments with marbled ware, and produced many teapots finished with brown and green streaked and mottled glazes. These are the ancestors of our ordinary 'kitchen teapots' of today. Whieldon took into partnership Josiah Wedgwood, who was to become the most famous of all English potters, and at their factories he made teapots of Jasper ware, that unglazed blue, pink, green, lilac, yellow or black stoneware, ornamented with classical subjects in white relief, with which the name of Wedgwood has come to be associated. The same firm has gone on making this ware ever since and it is still available today. But the pottery which Wedgwood perfected, and which was imitated by potters all over the country, was his Queen's Ware, a cream-coloured earthenware. The Queen's Ware teapots were graceful, classical shapes decorated with transfer designs or attractive severe little borders. The Leeds potteries also produced a cream-coloured earthenware, and many teapots of beautiful quality and design were made there. A characteristic of Leeds pottery is its extreme lightness of weight.

At potteries in Sunderland, Leeds and Swansea handsome lustre teapots were made for those who liked the look of silver but who could not afford the price. The makers of salt-glazed ware had derived much inspiration from the work of the silversmiths, and here again silverware had inspired the makers of the lustre-decorated pottery.

Porcelain was made on the Continent from about 1720 onwards at Meissen and then in other factories in Germany, Italy and France. The painting of flowers, fruit and birds on the Continental porcelain of Meissen and Sèvres was of a very high standard indeed. The English porcelain factory at Chelsea (founded in 1745) produced work of equal excellence. Porcelain teapots were also made at Bow, Worcester, Derby, Plymouth, Bristol, Longton Hall, Swansea, Nantgarw and Swinton (Rockingham). In about 1780, the last-mentioned factory made curious lidless teapots, which were filled from the bottom. They were constructed on the inkwell principle with a tapering spiral tube, running up from the hole in the base almost to the top of the pot. No doubt these 'puzzle' teapots caused much amusement and wonder in their time. The tea must have been brewed in another vessel and afterwards decanted into these curiosities, as it would never have been possible to remove the leaves.

The factories at Chelsea, Worcester and Lowestoft probably specialized more in tablewares than the other factories, and a great many styles of teapot were produced, with widely differing types of decoration. At Worcester, during the time when Dr Wall was running the factory (1751–1783), some of the finest table services were made. A Worcester teapot is shown on page 160. Most of the factories also made a few doll's tea services—fascinating miniatures of their larger originals. The porcelain painters of Staffordshire were never quite so skilful, and during the nineteenth century their work became heavier and more ornate. Pottery teapots also deteriorated in design and workmanship as more and more mass production methods were introduced into the industry, and the transfer-printed teapots of the late nineteenth century have little to recommend them.

An amusing example of mid-Victorian earthenware is the Queen Victoria Jubilee Commemoration teapot (shown on page 170). These pots were of a very large size, brown in colour with raised decorations in pink, white and blue. A most curious feature was the knob on the lid which was always surmounted with a tiny teapot, a perfect miniature of the larger pot. They were much used on the long-boats on the canals and have become known as 'barge teapots.'

Throughout the nineteenth century, English silversmiths were making teapots in silver. Although the workmanship was still good, the designs became heavier and more complicated as the Victorian craving for more and yet more decoration had to be satisfied.

Since Victorian times public taste has changed again and again. Weakly designed pastel-coloured teapots or *art nouveau* metal ones graced the Edwardian drawing-room. After the first world war came the age of 'jazz' and 'modernistic' designs, when teapots of triangular shape and unparalleled ugliness appeared. They were followed in the 1930's by unremarkable shapes, feeble posies, and concentric rings.

It is quite possible today to buy mass-produced earthenware and porcelain teapots of good design, that are pleasing to look at, comfortable to hold, and pour without spilling. Hand-made silver and hand-thrown pottery teapots of excellent design are obtainable today for those who wish—and do not mind paying the price for—something a little different.

Whatever happens to the price of tea, it seems likely that we shall continue to need teapots, for we shall not easily be broken of this long-established, pleasant and sociable habit.

[164]

AN ENGLISH FAMILY AT TEA
Detail from an oil-painting by an unknown artist
of the British School, *circa* 1720
Victoria and Albert Museum

Early English silver tea-pot inscribed with the arms of the East India Company, 1670–1 This is believed to be the oldest English silver pot. *Victoria and Albert Museum*

An example of fine salt-glazed stone ware for which Nottingham was famous in the eighteenth century. The date is about 1750. *Nottingham Museum and Art Gallery*

Red eighteenth-century Chinese
stone ware from Yi-Hsing
S. C. Ducrow Collection

Red Elers stone ware, copied from
the Chinese and made in Stoke-
on-Trent. *Circa* 1700,
Stoke-on-Trent Museum

Astbury ware. The white decorations are laid on a brownish black
body and covered with a thin lead
glaze. *Hanley Museum*

Agate ware, made by Thomas
Whieldon, *circa* 1750
Rev. C. J. Sharp Collection

Cauliflower teapot, made by
Thomas Whieldon, *circa* 1760
Tea Centre

Cream coloured earthenware teapot, probably made in Leeds,
circa 1800
Castle Museum, Norwich

Salt-glazed stoneware teapots from the collection of Miss Silk, and reproduced here by her kind permission. At the top, towards the centre, is a 'feather' pot. The one below shows a portrait medallion of Frederick the Great of Prussia (*c.* 1765)

Towards the centre, above, a 'Bonnie Prince Charlie' pot, showing the Prince in a pattern of oakleaves. The decoration on the teapot below, to the left, is embossed after the manner of Astbury ware. On the right are typical floral treatments

Early nineteenth-century earthenware teapot in the form of a Russian Bear with Napoleon in his grip. *Pitt Rivers Museum*

Queen Victoria's Diamond Jubilee Commemoration teapot. These were much used on long boats on the canals. *John Brinkley Colle*

Below : Teapot in the form of an elephant, in Oriental style, made by Ralph Wood, 1766 *C T Fowler Collection*

An early American teapot. Made by the famous silversmith William
Pollard of Boston, Mass. (1690–1746.) *John Bell Collection, Aberdeen*

Below : Contemporary silver teapot with laminated wood handle and chased and applied
decoration : designed by R. Y. Goodden, R.D.I., and made by Wakeley and Wheeler

Combinations and contrasts in shape and colour of foliage can make
the arrangement of leaves and branches as exciting and satisfying
as that of a bunch of flowers. The garden offers many opportunities ;
but for those who live in the country there is the delight of exploring
woods and hedgerows, rich in material at all times of the year

IN PRAISE OF FOLIAGE

by BETTY MASSINGHAM

Nor white nor red was ever seen
So am'rous as this lovely green.

ANDREW MARVELL, *The Garden*

 N THE WESTERN WORLD the demand for colour in decoration has often been interpreted by things vivid and bright and even garish. We have chosen bright flowers for our gardens—beds of Siberian wallflowers, lobelia, calceolarias and marigolds, and we have arranged our cut flowers to give a massed and colourful effect. The design of the garden generally, or the line of the flower arrangement, have often come as an afterthought.

The Orientals, on the other hand, have always realized the value of light and shade, and have shown appreciation of soft colours and tones, and of green in particular. The appreciation of foliage seems to depend very much on the value of green as a colour—of the different tones and shades which are possible within that colour. The opening lines of many verses in Chinese poetry have the words 'Green, green . . .'

Green, green, those elm-tree leaves . . .

Green, green, the grass by the river-bank . . .

Green, green—the grass of the Eastern Suburb ;
And amid the grass, a road that leads to the hills.

and

Green, green, the cypress on the mound . . .

With the exception of Arthur Hugh Clough, not many English poets seem to show such insistence on green as a colour. This may be because of the Eastern feeling for foliage generally and especially with reference to arrangement for indoor decoration. In almost any book on Japanese flower work much space is devoted to illustrations of camellia leaves, bamboo canes, and branches of maple, cedar, pine and willow. This seldom happens in English books. As Mr Josiah Conder says in his *Theory of Japanese Flower Arrangements* : 'The foliage of evergreens and other trees and plants is much used in *floral* composition, the arrangement often being without a single blossom.'

It is true that the Victorians dallied with the idea of using green, but only as something subsidiary to an arrangement. 'Green is essential in all bouquets,' writes a gardening editor of the period. 'Feathery and plumey green adds grace to all arrangements of flowers, and variegated foliage is exceedingly pretty for bordering baskets and flat dishes.' This suggests some, if rather limited, appreciation of leaves and ferns for use with flowers, but makes no suggestion of using them as the only decorative feature.

William Robinson, writing at the turn of the century, remarks on lessons already learnt from the Japanese in appreciation of form and line 'in a single twig or branch, with its natural habit shown, apart from any beauty and form or colour of its flowers.' This coincides with the ideas of Gertrude Jekyll at the time, but then they were two of the pioneers in simplicity and appreciation of the truth of natural things—ahead of their own time and, it seems, in many ways ahead of ours.

It is, then, a question of appreciation of line and tone and detail rather than the craving for the 'blaze of colour' beloved of the seed packets. 'Light and shade,' writes Arthur R. Howell, in *The Meaning and Purpose of Art*, 'are colour.' The demand for something bright, without any half-tones of light and shadow, is almost as crude as the belief that quantity is a sure expedient of a successful arrangement. When we consider the point carefully, 'it is doubtful if we like mere brightness in flowers any better than we do in people.' Mr Jason Hill, in *The Contemplative Gardener*, goes on to say : 'there is a great deal of beauty . . . if only we do not insist upon flowers and if we are willing to regard green and brown as colours.'

It may stir the imagination to recall the respect and esteem bestowed on leaves and evergreens in the past. It is well known that many of them were used for garlands and wreaths as marks of honour during the time of the Roman Empire—the Talmud mentions particularly that myrtle was used to deck Mohammedan tombs and coffins. Pliny mentions a certain plane tree that was so valued by the Romans that they cherished it 'by pouring wine upon it, it being found that the roots were greatly strengthened by doing so.' Vines, extravagantly well-nourished, grew to such heights that 'the vintager when hired was wont to stipulate for his funeral pile and a grave at the owner's expense.'

The leaves of Southwell show appreciation for the decorative design of foliage—the vine, maple, oak, ivy, hawthorn and hop, amongst others.

The particular reference to Sweet Bay—the Laurel sacred to Apollo —by Boccaccio, as a great honour for a queen is not surprising, nor, in our own era, the eulogy by Gertrude Jekyll : 'Of all the lovely forms of branch and leaf, the one that may be said to be of extremest beauty —that of the Sweet Bay—may be enjoyed in winter. To anyone who has a keen delight in the beauty of form, that of a twig of Bay is little less than amazing.' She goes on to describe the shape and texture of its leaf : '. . . the whole structure showing the most admirable design for strength and beauty, grace and refinement—is truly a thing to marvel at, and to have and hold with the utmost reverence and thankfulness.'

Perhaps here lies the secret. Respect for green growing things is not anything new ; it is rather something we have lost sight of, and which we should do well to recover. Dürer managed to find excitement and interest in a small patch of green turf, resulting in a painting full of tender detail and love for the small things of nature.

In our zeal for art and originality we may be inclined to overlook the truth and beauty of natural things. Plato held that 'the greatest and the fairest things are done by nature and the lesser by Art.' Sometimes it seems as though ordinary observance is dulled and blunted and only something outstanding in colour or shape or size qualifies for notice. And all the time there are the soft shades and beautiful shapes, deep tones and architectural structures of leaf and branch to be seen and appreciated and used.

William Robinson had some stern things to say about the general attitude to art and nature. '. . . we live n a time of much printed fog about artistic things—the "New Art" and the "New Aesthetic" ; "Evolution," which explains how everything comes from nothing and goes back again to worse than nothing ; the sliding bog of "realism and idealism" in which the phrasemonger may dance around and say the same false thing ten times over ; . . . art is of many kinds, and owing to the confusion caused in many minds by the loose "critical" talk of the day, it is not easy for all to see that true art is based on clear-eyed study and love of nature, rather than on the invention and the "personality" of the artist of which we hear so much.' (*The Garden Beautiful.*) He was writing about fifty years ago, but he was ahead of his time, and if he were writing today might find little to alter in this paragraph.

Perhaps it is the microscopic eye which should be cultivated ; the eye which is capable of seeing detail which does not at once scream

[175]

out for recognition. Perhaps, too, as Gertrude Jekyll says, when we have found our leaf or twig or branch or bud, we should hold it 'with the utmost reverence and thankfulness.'

> In the night of the chestnut, by the chestnut candles
> Burning, red and white, upon the lowest boughs ;
> We will lie and listen for a god to come.
> What is that glitter from the ilex-trees,
> For the leaves flash like armour in a torch-lit night :
> What is this sweetness from the myrtle-wood ?*

It is interesting to experiment in arousing this perception and vision in the smallest things by studying with a completely new approach something which we consider to be quite ordinary—to look closely, for instance, into a rosette of London Pride, or a spray of ivy-leafed Toadflax growing on a cottage wall ; to examine carefully a clump of velvet moss, or a trail of clear-pointed, dark, shining Ivy. These often live their life through with little recognition, because we are so sure of them. Mr Jason Hill quotes another case in point : 'We know so surely that the clump of Fennel will reappear where it was planted, that the sculptural beauty of its sea-green columnar stems and the moulding of its pale bracts usually develops and passes unnoticed.'

In flower and foliage arrangement, it is the line of the arrangement which is the expression of the arranger more than any other part of the composition. The colour of the flowers, or the flowers themselves, convey different impressions, depending on the interests of whoever is looking at them. A bunch of roses seen in a flower shop by, say, a housewife, a young man, a gardener and a florist, delights all four of them, arousing at the same time quite different ideas in each one of them. The housewife would like some to arrange in her house, the young man would like one for a buttonhole, the gardener would like a cutting, and the florist decides to find out the name and order some for his own shop. It is not, therefore, the material or the colour of a flower or foliage arrangement which is going to produce a unanimous reaction : only a particular one. It is the line and design of the group which can have only one interpretation, as it is the original thought of the arranger which has produced it. The flower and the colour are there for the asking, but it is the arranger's idea of design which has evolved the shape of the arrangement, and which makes it unique.

Beautiful and glorious and necessary as colour is to life, we may come

* *Canons of Giant Art*, Sacheverell Sitwell.

Variegated Periwinkle arranged in an early glass jug with Clematis
(Comtesse de Bouchard). The curving stems of Periwinkle and the turns
and twists of Clematis leaf-stalks are invaluable for flower arrangement.

Globe artichoke leaves provide an interesting background for branches of berried St John's Wort, a cluster of acorns and a few pieces of heather turned golden brown.

Cotoneaster with Laurel. The Portugal Laurel, Aucuba and Sweet Bay all provide useful evergreen contrasts to smaller and more 'cut-out' foliage such as Cotoneaster—or Lonicera.

Branches of Sea Buckthorn, Horse Radish leaves and Hop flowers arranged in a baking tin. The rather severe lines of cooking dishes seem particularly suitable to foliage.

Shining, dark green Ivy interlaced through branches of Escallonia. Ivy is one of the most beautiful and useful materials for winter flower decoration.

Eucalyptus arranged in a sage and white Victorian vase. The shape and colour of the leaves, slightly reminiscent of Honesty seedpods when green, make this foliage very exciting material to use.

to understand that it 'becomes significant only when it has been made subservient to form.'*

The importance of design in English flower arrangement can hardly be over-estimated. A flower group in Japan is one of only two or three objects in the room. It shares, probably with a scroll picture, space in an alcove built especially for it which is the focus-point of the room. In England, the importance of an arrangement is of quite a different kind. Its function is to combine with the decorative scheme of the furnishings, of which there are usually many in great variety. And so the design of the group becomes part of the room and an integral part of the *décor*. Half the value of an English flower arrangement is its suitability for fitting into its setting : for maintaining the balance of the room—not being too important, but important enough.

The design of a Japanese flower arrangement is based on symbolism, and that of an English flower arrangement on its position in the furnishing scheme.

The possibilities of using foliage in this country are certainly no less than in Japan, and to explore them opens up new fields in home floral decoration. It must, I think, be agreed that foliage decorations offer a wide scope in the development of design, and that it is possible, by the use of contrasting shapes of leaves, to obtain interesting effects in line arrangements. In the matter of contrast it is as though one type of leaf takes the place of the flower in the group and the other acts as a background or a setting for it by virtue of its distinctive shape or colour.

Most branches are, in themselves, dramatic or graceful in shape or line. If they are arranged as far as possible in their natural position they will show off to their best advantage. It is usually quite unnecessary to bend or twist them or to try to improve in any way on their usual growth. There are, perhaps, two exceptions where one may be forgiven for using the leaves back to front, which is, after all, a small distortion. The elegant tan-coloured backs of magnolia grandiflora look well if arranged against their own dark green, and the soft silver-grey of rosemary leaves can only be seen effectively when used the wrong way round.

It is difficult to know where to begin to enumerate the different leaves and branches particularly suitable for decoration. Perhaps it would be as well to go through the seasons of the year.

Art, Clive Bell

In winter there are long sprays of periwinkle—dark and shiny or variegated, branches of ilex, sweet bay, Portugal laurel, camellia green, grevillea, variegated holly, eucalyptus, deep red branches of dogwood, holly, ivy, and clusters of 'pale-green, fairy mistletoe.'

In the spring all the fruit tree branches are coming into flowering bud and a particularly beautiful one, if it can be spared, is a branch of quince. There are wild arum leaves, berberis in fresh green shoots, flowering currant, budding viburnum, pussy willow and catkins, larch, silver-grey shoots of whitebeam, Corsican hellebore and the dark, fan-like clusters of *Andromeda Pieris* foliage. A branch of budding chestnut is, of course, one of the most dramatic additions to an arrangement that it is possible to find. Purple sprouting broccoli and the rather knobbly, brown branches of sea buckthorn make an exciting contrast.

Summer-time is overflowing with suggestions, and one can only mention a few possibilities. *Stachys lanata*, garden ragwort, giant cow parsnip, globe artichoke, *funkia grandiflora*, privet, fennel, horse radish, hart's tongue fern, vine, everlasting pea, summer jasmine and iris. (This list is given, of course, only with reference to the foliage and not to the flowers.)

In the autumn there is a surprising selection. Forsythia and azalea both achieve very beautiful autumn colourings, *andromeda axillaris* is well known, and there are also scarlet oaks, varied *megasea*, clematis, *garrya elliptica* with its grey-green catkins, polypoddy fern, broom and golden privet, magnolia and ivy, rosemary and deep-toned berberis.

There are many more, and as I write I think all the time of yet another one ; but quite half the delight and enjoyment is to discover interesting and exciting shapes and colours of leaves for oneself, so I will be content with an incomplete list.

THE UNCONDUCTED ORCHESTRA

by CONSTANTINE BENCKENDORFF

N THE AUTUMN of 1922 I found myself at a loose end in
Moscow. I had resigned from the Russian Navy,
where a rather spectacular career on the General
Staff had been abruptly cut short by a few brushes
with the security people. In a world sorely depleted
for me by the emigration of nearly all my friends and
relations I found myself drawn towards a set of people who, up
till then, had been practically *terra incognita*. They were musicians.

Music had always been—and still is—one of the chief pleasures in
my life ; but this fact had not been recognized by my family. At the
age of twelve I had won in a tombola a specimen of what is commonly
known as a three-quarter flute—something between a grand and a
piccolo, which is still used, I believe, in military bands. Day after day
I had practised on it, and I had spent nearly all my pocket money on
reams of flute music, most of it far beyond my capacity. Gradually I
had come to be what I fondly imagined was a full-blown flautist,
capable of tackling any score. I had carried my flutes with me everywhere. Through the bombardment of Port Arthur and the Arctic
gales of Murmansk their shriek had been heard by friend and foe.
My only setback had been the loss of the most beloved of all, a rosewood
Moenig of incomparable tone and beauty.

And now, by force of circumstance and the Bolshevik *coup d'état*,
I found myself exchanging the society of country gentlemen and naval
officers for that of composers, singers and professional instrumentalists
—a highly congenial set of friends, who, like myself, had not been
brought up to toil with their hands.

By chance I entered this new and exciting world just in time to take
part in a remarkable scheme which was born in the fertile brain of
Professor Zeitlin, a violinist of international distinction, an orchestral
leader of unsurpassed experience, and a noted teacher of his instrument.

Having played many times under world-known conductors Zeitlin
questioned the necessity of a body of experienced players being directed
by those gentlemen at a performance. Any well-rehearsed orchestra,
he contended, should get the hang of the conductor's interpretation at
rehearsal, and should have no need of a conductor at the actual

performance. Indeed he considered that without a conductor they should even be able to improve on his interpretation.

Who, he would argue, ever heard of a stage performance during which a producer ran about on the stage and gave the actors continuous indications of the interpretation of their roles ? And yet what was the difference between a stage production and an orchestral performance ? Musicians even have the advantage of their parts before them, with no need for a prompter. The musical score gives more and subtler indications of how it should be performed than the book of a play, and these every orchestral player ought to be able to interpret. In Zeitlin's view conductors ought to retire after the final rehearsal and let the orchestra perform undirected, for he insisted that in these days of fully trained musicians the only role left to the conductor was the interpretation of the work to the audience by his gestures.

It was Zeitlin's view—shared, I admit, by most orchestral players— that even a composer had little to give to an orchestra in performance. Indeed, some of the greatest composers, such as Debussy and Tchaikovsky, have been frankly terrible conductors.

So many conductors are given to unclear and fuzzy signalisation, both in time and in emphasis. Their use of unconventional gestures is meaningless and merely distracts attention. A further argument of Zeitlin's was that the conductor's gestures, intended to moderate or increase sound, must necessarily come too late for effect, as he has to hear what is wrong before he can correct it.

All that was necessary, according to Zeitlin's theory, was to place the players so that they could watch each other, as in chamber music.

Whatever the merits of Zeitlin's theory, the idea found immediate and enthusiastic support amongst the members of the State Theatre's orchestras, nearly all of them teachers at the Moscow Conservatoire. A co-operative society called the 'First Conductorless Symphonic Ensemble'—for short, Persimfans—was created and a series of concerts in the Grand Hall of the Conservatoire decided upon at the first general meeting.

Now, in those days of renewed possibilities for private enterprise a certain capital for initial expenses was necessary. This was where I came in: I happened to be able to provide it. The sum required, though it ran into millions of roubles, was in reality only the equivalent of £10 to £15 in gold, and I had this amount left over from the sale of a cigarette case on the Black Market. (To illustrate the value of currency

[184]

in those days I recall that a concert harp of one of the best makes, in perfect condition, and still in constant use today in England, changed hands for 40 pounds of salt, 4 yards of cloth, 15 yards of silk, and a million roubles, the money being an insignificant item in the transaction.)

Having produced my capital I was elected to the Board of Directors of the Persimfans, which had Zeitlin as Chairman. Furthermore, I was permitted to take the part of third flute in those rare works where composers have included that number in their score, unmindful of Mozart's opinion of the depressing effect that such prodigality was to produce.

More than sufficient distinguished players and a large number of advanced pupils of the Conservatoire volunteered to give as much time to rehearsals as was required, and a large symphonic orchestra came into being. At the first concert a hit was scored with the Moscow public. A representative selection from a classical, romantic and contemporary repertoire was performed, and the performances were unquestionably of outstanding merit. Soloists, both vocal and instrumental, freely admitted that the accompaniment was as good as they desired.

The keystone of conductorless playing was the disposition of the executants on the platform. To the audience the orchestra presented an unusual sight. Upstage the backs of all the first and second violins were to be seen, arranged in a semi-circle. At either side were the violas and the cellos. The double basses closed the formation backstage, and faced the audience. The woodwind and brass formed concentric circles within this outer formation, all facing one another, with the percussion in a group in front of the double basses. There was a small platform for soloists in the centre.

This disposition was necessary to enable all the leaders and most of the players to have a clear view of each other, and not lose sight of the leading first violin, who sat in the middle of the front segment. Zeitlin himself was the leading first violin, and, in spite of his original assumption that during rehearsals a conductor would take charge and 'produce' his own interpretation, it was the indefatigable Zeitlin himself who 'produced' all the programmes from the beginning to the end of that first series of concerts.

It was a most impressive moment when, at a performance, the slight preliminary tap of Zeitlin's bow silenced a group of sometimes up to a hundred players and a huge expectant audience. Only a few of that audience would notice Zeitlin's bow raised a few inches before an imperceptible signal was given and the music of the whole orchestra miraculously materialized.

The orchestra followed with uncanny precision every phrase and mood of the soloists, always supporting and never obscuring them— and that for the most obvious reason, that if they overplayed they would be the first not to hear the soloists and thus lose touch with them.

For myself it was a wonderful experience, though sometimes an unnerving one for a player entirely inexperienced in orchestral work. I remember one morning when Persimfans was rehearsing an excerpt from Wagner. The three flutes had just entered a long-drawn chord in the lower register, of which my part demanded from me the lowest note. The first violins, facing us not a yard away, were playing a fast-moving figuration in accompaniment when I heard Zeitlin's voice, as he scraped away vigorously on his fiddle, muttering 'Oh, what a horrible G flat ! What a horrible G flat !' Of course, the G flat was mine : my own ear had been warning me this was so, but Zeitlin's mutterings were too much for me, and the chord had to continue without the G flat Wagner intended.

But I was not always alone in my discomfiture. Our side-drummer, an ancient, meek little man, who had been wielding his sticks for not less than a half-century, could not straighten out a certain rhythmical figure in Rimsky-Korsakov's *Scheherezade*, which somehow went wrong every time. When the orchestra had come to a stop half a dozen times the plaintive voice of the old man became audible : 'But, Mr Zeitlin, it was Alexander Sergeech (that is, Rimsky-Korsakov) *himself* who taught me to play this as I do.'

Whether or not the unconducted orchestra was a symptom of a supposedly egalitarian way of life, or merely a child of Zeitlin's brain, I do not know. Certainly years afterwards Persimfans was still going strong in Moscow, and I believe that quite a number of other Simfanses, with the suitable numeral prefixed, were formed in other parts of Russia. One hears little of them now. Is this because they have disappeared ? Certainly the sweeping change in orchestral practice which we envisaged in those far-off days has not come about. But I still think there is more to be said for it than against, even in a capitalist country.

THE BAGPIPE

by SETON GORDON

HE ORIGIN of the bagpipe is lost in the mists of antiquity, for the wind instrument is probably the earliest form of music. Popular opinion links the bagpipe with the Scottish Highlands, but almost every country of the world had this instrument, in various forms. There are, it is said, Chaldean sculptures of about 4000 B.C. with a representation of the pipes. The ancient Egyptians and Persians played on them. There is a legend that the shepherds watching their flocks on the night of Christ's birth played their bagpipes at Bethlehem in their joy at the birth of their Lord. Sixty years later the Roman emperor Nero vowed that if he should escape death at the hands of his enemies he would perform on the bagpipe (*utricularis*) at the public games. Even before Nero's day, 'nine pipers from the fairy hills of Bregia' came to play to Conaire the Great, High King of Eire, whose time was around 35 B.C.

In England there are early records of pipers. In 1307, in the reign of Edward II, there is the record of two payments to a bagpiper named Janino Chrevretter who played before the king. The term 'Chevrette' means a bagpipe with a deerskin bag. Chaucer wrote :

> A bagpipe well could he blow and sound
> And therewithal he brought us out of town.

Queen Elizabeth's band of music in 1587 included a bagpiper

Although the primitive bagpipe was universal, it was in the Highlands and islands of Scotland that the instrument and its music evolved to their highest form. The oldest known Highland bagpipe was in the possession of the late Mr Glen, of Edinburgh. This pipe has two drones, which have a common base. Near their base is the date MCCCCIX, or 1409. This pipe may have been played at the Battle of Harlaw, fought north of Aberdeen in 1411. The bagpipe was then popular in Scotland, and it is said that King James I of that country was a tolerable piper. It was a century or rather more after this that the greatest pipers of all time, the MacCrimmons, began to be talked of. One of the most notable of this celebrated family was Donald Mór

MacCrimmon, who composed *MacDonald's Salute, MacLeod's Rowing Pibroch*, and others. These tunes, composed around the year 1600, are still considered among the finest pieces of classical pipe music.

At that time there were apparently three different forms of bagpipe in Scotland—the Highland Pipe, the Lowland Pipe, and the Irish Pipe. In a Highland MS. known as the Bannatyne Manuscript is a poem written by Alexander Hume, Minister of Logie, on the relief felt in Scotland on the defeat of the Armada of Spain. Hume writes that 'Hieland pipes, Scottes, and Hybernicke' should all join in the nation's thanksgiving. The celebrated MacCrimmons played on the 'Hieland pipes,' known usually as the Piob Mhór or Great Pipe. In Dunvegan Castle, that strong castle of the MacLeod chiefs in the Isle of Skye, is preserved what is reputed to be the bagpipe played by Patrick Mór MacCrimmon, son of Donald Mór. This pipe is named Piob Bhreac. The tops of the three drones are all that remain of the original instrument. The fact that this old set of pipes has three drones is of unusual interest to pipers, because it has been generally supposed that the third or big drone is comparatively modern. But Joseph MacDonald, the first man who wrote about piping, in his *Compleat Theory of the Scots Highland Bagpipe*, a treatise compiled *circa* 1760, states that in his time the pipers of the west Highlands, as opposed to those of the north Highlands, had 'laid aside the use of the great Drone' because 'the loudness of it drowned the sound of the Chanter music.' This would seem to account for the fact that the pipe of Iain Dubh MacCrimmon, whose time was *circa* 1784, which is also to be seen in Dunvegan Castle, has no great drone. The MacCrimmons on innumerable occasions must have played in the Castle of Dunvegan, for they were the hereditary pipers to the MacLeods of Dunvegan.

At this time, and much later, another form of the bagpipe was in use in the Highlands. This may be the pipe referred to by Hume as 'Scottes.' The Gaelic name for this pipe is Piob Shionnaich, the Bellows Pipe. This pipe is not the same as the Irish Piob Uillean or Elbow Pipe, which Shakespeare, having no knowledge of Gaelic, names the 'woollen' pipe ! Angus Macpherson, a celebrated piper and a judge of piping at the great Highland Gatherings, tells me that in his family there is preserved his father's Piob Shionnaich. His father, Malcolm Macpherson, was a famous piper—his photograph is one of the illustrations of this article—and, like his father before him, was

A modern bagpipe, with unusually attractive carving, the property of Mr Cameron-Head, of Inverailort. *Below*, the scale for the bagpipe, taken from Angus Mackay's *Collection of Ancient Piobaireachd or Highland Pipe Music*, 1838.

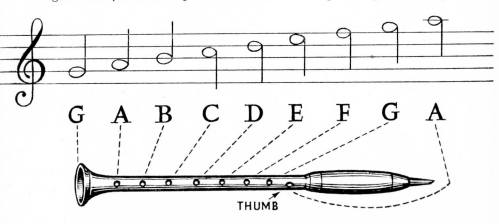

A piper celebrated at the turn of the century was Malcolm Macpherson, piper to Cluny MacPherson of Cluny, and father of Angus Macpherson, now a judge of piping at the great Highland Gatherings. On the right is one of the most brilliant pipers of the younger generation, Donald Macpherson (he is no relation of Angus Macpherson).

A group of famous pipers on a yacht off Dunvegan, in the Isle of Skye, in 1933. *Left to right :* Pipe Major Robert Reid, Pipe Major John MacDonald, of Inverness—by universal consent the most celebrated piper of his day, Sir Reginald MacLeod of MacLeod, and Angus Macpherson of Invershin.

man MacRae, piper for nearly 50 years to Sir Donald Cameron of Lochiel, photographed by grave of Charles MacKarter, piper to Macdonald of the Isles in the eighteenth century.

great piper of nearly a hundred rs ago was Sandy MacDonald, ate manager and piper to Macpherson Glentrum. The photograph above s taken in Paris about 1873. On the ht is the author, Mr Seton Gordon.

Piob Shionnaich played by the pipers of Sir Alexander Cameron's company of the Rifle Brigade on its formation. The bag is filled by a bellows and not by the piper's breath.

equally at home, and equally skilled, on either type of bagpipe. In those days dances would be continued for several nights in succession, and the piper, having opened the proceedings with the Great Pipe, would then sit at his ease on a stool or bench, and play dance music on the Bellows Pipe hour after hour, the fingering and scale in both Piob Mhór and Piob Shionnaich being the same.

The illustration of the Piob Shionnaich here reproduced was given me by Francis Cameron-Head of Inverailort. Three pipes of this type have long been in the possession of the Inverailort family. The bag covers are Rifle Brigade green; the chanters are sweet and musical; the drone reeds are smaller than in the Piob Mhór. The bellows, which are worked by the player's elbow, can be seen in the illustration. The background of the photograph is a Cameron tartan plaid, which has been in the Inverailort family for more than a hundred years.

In the modern Highland bagpipe of three drones the great drone is an octave lower than the two tenor drones. The bag is of sheepskin, with an outer cover of blue or green velvet, or of tartan cloth. It is held usually under the left arm so that the right, or sword arm, is free. The chanter has the scale of an octave and one note—from low G to high A. The scale is fixed and cannot be altered in any way : the intervals, it is said, are different from those of any other known scale. The chanter reeds and the drone reeds are of cane. The chanter reed is strong and shrill ; none but a piper has any idea of the difficulty in acquiring a really good chanter reed : a true and melodious reed, not too exhausting to blow, is beyond price. The drone reeds, which produce a steady hum, are less of a problem than the chanter reed, but clear and steady drone reeds are not easy to come by ; a common defect is what is known as 'roaring.' The piper fills his bag with wind through a blowpipe. A steady flow of sound is maintained by a gradual pressure of the piper's arm to supply the reeds with air while he, in the words of an old book, 'is fetching another draught.' The same book emphasises that in blowing 'the cheek must be kept firmly contracted, with a smile on the countenance, in a free and manly posture, and not twisting the body nor disfiguring the face, which are disgusting.'

Modern Highland bagpipes are made from foreign wood. Pipe Major Robert Reid, a piper of renown, and head of a large piping business in Glasgow, which he built up himself, has given me notes on the timbers used in bagpipe making. (1) African Blackwood. Reputedly the best and most vibrant. Dark brown in colour. Favoured by most manufacturers at the present day. (2) Ebony. Not quite so popular nowadays, and good quality is in short supply. A very good, vibrant timber, but is short in the grain, which makes breakages possible. Colour, bluish-black. (3) Cocus Wood. A very good, vibrant wood. Colour light brown, with a beautiful natural grain. Its light colour is not too popular among pipers. (4) Mocambese Ebony—this is better known as Partridgewood. A vibrant wood and long in the grain and therefore tough. A popular wood for the bagpipe at the present time. All these timbers are expensive—between £40 and £50 per ton in log form before being sawn and prepared by the purchaser. The price includes bark and waste—considerable items in weight. It is said that at one time native Highland timber was used in the making of bagpipes, and that holly was favoured. In the making of the bagpipe the turning and boring of the wood is always done by hand and is highly skilled work.

The music of the Highland bagpipe or Piob Mhór may be grouped under three headings. (1) Ceòl Mór, the Great Music. This may be said to be the Classical Pipe Music. (2) Ceòl Beag, the Little Music. Marches (including the highly specialized Competition Marches), Strathspeys and Reels belong to this class. (3) Ceòl Meadhonach, the Middle Music—middle, that is, between the last two groups—consisting of Slow Marches and of Highland airs adapted to the bagpipe.

The notation of pipe music is now staff notation, but up to a century and a half ago Ceòl Mór was imparted to the pupil by the teacher in the form of Canntaireachd. The ground of the tune and the different measures following the ground were sung by the teacher. In Canntaireachd each part of the tune has a special symbol. This symbol is present in each group of syllables which stand for groups of notes, grace notes included.

Even in the Highlands of Scotland scarcely one person in a thousand has real knowledge of pipe music. Many people believe that powerful lungs are the chief necessity to make a piper. Actually one's bagpipe should be so easy to blow that this is done without effort, and one's concentration may be wholly focused in one's fingering and flow of melody. There is much musical talent and hard work necessary in the making of a good piper. It was not without reason that the MacCrimmons of Skye required a residence of seven years at their piping school at Borreraig by those who came from Scotland, and even from Eire, to be taught by them.

I recall travelling to London with the late Pipe Major John MacDonald, M.B.E., of Inverness, by almost universal consent the greatest piper of the last fifty years, in order that he might record tunes for the Columbia Gramophone Company. I do not think that up to then (this was some ten years after the close of the first world war) any records had been made of Ceòl Mór, the classical pipe music. Those who did the recording did not profess to know the first thing about piping, and it was most interesting to me to see how John MacDonald impressed on them his personality and the skill and beauty of his playing. Now that the great piper has gone, these records are of almost priceless value, for the matrix has been destroyed.

There are many points by which the skilled piper's music can be distinguished. First, there is the quality of chanter and drone reeds, which must not only be themselves excellent but must be well tuned. Each of the drones has movable slides. After a few minutes' playing the warm, moist breath of the pipe causes the chanter reed to become sharper : this necessitates the tuning down of the slides of the drones. In a competition it is of great importance that the piper should know his reeds well. There is a longer or shorter period, during which he is tuning 'off-stage' before playing, while the reeds are 'tuning down' or are unsteady. There is then a period while the pitch remains constant. The piper says to himself, 'My pipes are steady.' He then mounts the platform, hoping that his pipes may remain steady until the end of his tune. If the pipes 'go off' (become out of tune) in the middle of his piece, his chances of a prize are small, however well he may be playing. The reader must remember that the piper cannot stop for even the fraction of a second during his performance to adjust the slides of his drones, nor is it permitted for a friend to do this for him.

A piece of classical pipe music takes anything from ten to twenty-two minutes to play. Besides the art of having perfectly tuned and steady reeds during all that time, a considerable test of memory is required. The piper has no score of music before him ; his tune must be well and truly memorized. He may have to submit to the judges a list of twelve difficult tunes, any one of which he might be called on to play.

In addition to having true and musical reeds the piper must see to it that the bag of his pipe is soft and supple and thoroughly airtight. The quality of the skin of the bag is most important—old pipers insisted on the skin of a three-year-old wedder sheep for this purpose. In order that the bag be airtight, a mixture of white-of-egg and brown sugar, diluted by hot water, is poured into the bag and worked carefully by the hands into the seams and every part of it. The size of the pipe bag varies with the piper's taste. There is a standard size, but some of the most notable pipers have used a bag considerably larger than the average. The larger the bag (within reason) the steadier the blowing. Angus Macpherson and John MacDonald have favoured a large bag.

But an indifferent piper cannot play well on the most perfectly tuned pipe having the softest and most airtight bag. In pipe music, and especially in classical pipe music, the master player is recognized after even a few notes. He has rhythm, correct timing and phrasing, and the ability to finger the grace notes (these form an important part of pipe music) so swiftly and so correctly that, in the words of a very great piper, they produce a ripple, as from the strings of a harp. Delicacy and accuracy of touch ; giving the theme notes their full value ; the ability to string the tune together—-these, and other points, distinguish the master player. Yet, more important than all, is his ability, because of his gift of music, to awaken the soul or spirit of a tune. Watch the reaction of the judges and the critical audience at the great piping events of the Northern Meeting at Inverness. See their sudden concentration when some player, perhaps hitherto little known, is shaping well on the platform. See how they follow his clear notes as he passes from one variation to another, and, if his playing goes from strength to strength, how they sit spellbound during the final and most intricate variations—the Crunlaudh with its doubling and tripling.

How, it may be asked, is the young piper of the present day taught to acquit himself worthily in these great and nerve-shattering competitions ? For many years a six months' course of piping has been held each winter at Edinburgh Castle under the auspices of the Piobaireachd Society, for army pipers. The instructor, ever since the year 1919, has been Pipe Major William Ross, M.B.E., late of the Scots Guards—he whom the Press has named 'the world's pipe major.' This modest and kindly man, a great player indeed, has taught many champion pipers, and his skill becomes no less with the passing of the years. The Scots Guards have recently published a book of pipe music, and in it one classical piece takes the place of honour : It is *Salute to Pipe Major William Ross*, composed by his old friend and fellow competitor, Angus Macpherson of Invershin, angler, piper, author and dancer.

THE TREE AND THE CAMERA

Photographs by CLARENCE JOHN LAUGHLIN

The illustrations which follow are an attempt to show how the photographer—in just as real a sense as the creative painter—can find in nature images of fear and delight, and can see in, for instance, tree forms, correspondences to the arts of man himself. Emotionally some of these photographs are related to the paintings of Bosch, of James Ensor, Grandville or Paul Klee. Whilst ostensibly recording a natural scene the photographer has tried to hint at things which cannot be exactly measured, or completely known.

M^{\circledast}

TREE MOCKING A WOODPECKER

This, one of the famous cypress trees at Point Lobos, California, has
not only evolved a parody of the woodpeckers which torment it, but
has grown a miniature tree out of itself for the creature to peck at.

KING LEAR

In this study of a huge dead cypress tree in North Louisiana there is
an air of bitter and tragic grandeur. With its tortured limbs and its
twisted crown the battered tree suggested to the eye of the camera the
tragic figure of King Lear.

LITTLE FRIGHTENED GHOST

When the cypress trees of Louisiana are charred by fire they acquire
a surface of an incredibly rich and velvety black. Within the world
of such a partially burnt tree the photographer found a small uncharred
area—a little, gentle, timid ghost, whose image is dedicated to the
memory of Paul Klee.

PIGEON IN A TREE

The huge oak is dead ; yet it still seems to move with some serene
and secret life. A diagonal movement is balanced against a vertical
movement, accentuated, or modified, by the movements of the clouds.
The pigeon, alive but so inconspicuous, indicates the massive scale.

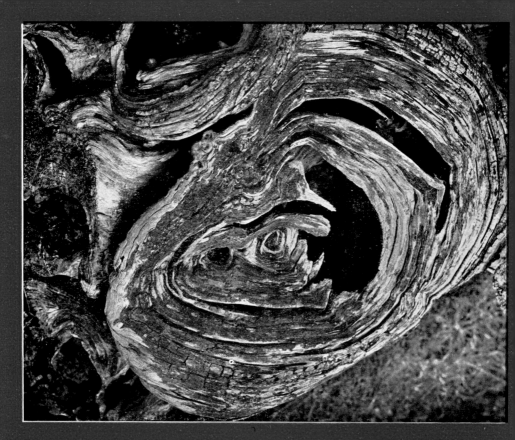

TREE INTO GOOSE

Opposite:

THE OLD
MAN OF
THE
WOOD

THE SECRET FACES OF FEAR

The bark and branch studies opposite are simple and recognizable.
Here, in the close-up of the tree-trunk above, we can discover at least
four strange, hardly definable monsters—perhaps more. Demonic,
reptilian, prehistoric? Surely these are the secret faces of our fears.

THE SOCIAL HISTORY OF
THE SWAN

by ERIC ST. JOHN BROOKS

Mysterious, beautiful ;
Among what rushes will they build,
By what lake's edge or pool
Delight men's eyes when I awake some day
To find they have flown away ?

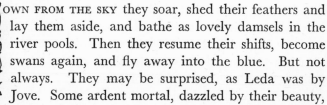OWN FROM THE SKY they soar, shed their feathers and lay them aside, and bathe as lovely damsels in the river pools. Then they resume their shifts, become swans again, and fly away into the blue. But not always. They may be surprised, as Leda was by Jove. Some ardent mortal, dazzled by their beauty, may steal the shift of the fairest and refuse to return it till she promises to wed him. This is the motive of a folk-tale common, in one form or another, to all the peoples of the world. There is another fairly constant feature in these tales. The fortunate husband of the captive swan-maiden must be careful to hide the shift which he has stolen, for if his wife should find it, she will don it again, resume her swan-shape, and fly away for good.

These swan-maidens, we are to understand, have been compelled by enchantment to take bird form. In Grimm's 'Six Swans,' the theme of which Hans Andersen elaborated, the wicked stepmother, by her magic, changes eleven princes into swans. Eliza, their sister, escaping from the witch's spells, sets forth to seek them. Wandering through the wood, she knows that they cannot be far off, for an old woman (a disguised fairy) tells her that she has seen eleven swans swimming in the river, and she herself finds eleven white swan-feathers on the foam-covered grass by the sea. Evening comes, and the swans appear, alighting and flapping their great white wings. Their feathers fall off, and lo ! they are handsome princes once more.

This, however, can only take place at nightfall. By day they are swans, who must fly in the sky unceasingly. Moreover, they must not be found at evening away from land, as, turned again into men, they must find, like Noah's dove, a spot of earth for the soles of their feet. As they cross the sea, an island or even a rock will suffice for their landfall. Only once a year may they revisit their old home, at the time when the days are longest, for it takes two days to fly across the rough seas to a rock where they spend the first night.

This time, when they return, the brothers take Eliza with them, borne in a net which they weave of willow-bark and reeds. They reach the tiny rock just as the sun is setting, and here as men they pass the night, crowded and weary with the wild seas and winds that beset them, until morning releases them, and they continue as swans their journey to the far land where they dwell. Here comes to Eliza the old fairy who had first told her of the eleven crowned swans. Now she tells Eliza how the charm that binds her brothers may be broken. She must weave eleven shirts from the nettles that burn and blister her fair hands and bare feet. And so finally the spell is broken, though in her haste Eliza has to leave a sleeve unfinished, so that the youngest brother retains a swan's wing in place of an arm.

Andersen, who embroiders the tale, as is his wont with other incidents, drew his main idea from the great body of European folklore. In Ireland, a story with similar features has been made famous by many poets and prose writers. This is the 'Tale of the Children of Lir.' Three boys, Aedh, Fiachra and Conn, and a girl, Fionnuala, are transformed into swans by their wicked stepmother. Their fate is harder than that of Andersen's children, for they remain swans, though there is granted to them the power of speech—'the sweet Gaelic speech'—and of song. For three hundred years they live on Lake Derryvarragh in Westmeath. For three hundred more years they fly around the Maoil, that is the Mull of Kintyre, gaining a foothold in their flights—as in Andersen's tale—on Carraig-na-Ron, the rock of the seals, suffering from the harsh winds and frozen seas. For a last three hundred years they dwell near the island of Achill. Not till then are their troubles ended, and then they are old, withered beings, who die after a saint has baptized them and effected their release. This piteous tale has secured the belief in many parts of Ireland that it is unlucky to kill a swan.

Tom Moore has celebrated one incident in this story, in the poem 'The Song of Fionnuala,' but of all the poems about the fate of the Children of Lir, I like best the youthful verses of Douglas Hyde, who did so much to bring about the Gaelic revival—the rebirth of 'the

sweet Gaelic speech' of which the tale tells.   Here we read of the
sorrows of 'the snowy-breasted four' ; and, as the swans sing,

> The liquid notes gushed in a golden stream
> Into the sky and flooded Darvra's shores
> With heavenly harmony, and all the air
> Grew heavy with the lingering liquid sound.
> The lark left singing of her evening song,
> Poised in the air she listened, and the thrush
> Ceased from his carol on the greenwood bough . . .

Thus the tale touches on another feature of swan lore—the bird's
singing, heard most often at the approach of death. Although our own
native bird, the 'mute swan,' is voiceless, we have a winter visitant,
the whooper or whistling swan, a native of Iceland and the northern
parts of Europe. In autumn and winter he wanders farther south, so
that his musical note has even been celebrated by Homer.

Sir James Frazer records an Icelandic tale in which a poor maiden
sets forth to seek a lost prince. She finds him in a cave, asleep, lying
upon a bed spread with a golden coverlet. He has been bewitched by
two hideous giantesses, one of whom wakes him from time to time to
propose marriage, which he indignantly refuses. In the cave are two
swans, and the prince's awakening is effected by the birds singing at
the command of the ogress :

> Sing, sing my swans,
> That the king's son may wake.

The hidden girl learns the secret, and wakes the prince. By her
contrivance the giantesses meet their death, and no doubt the prince,
who had refused the hand of the sorceress, marries his deliverer.

The tale of the enchanted swan has attracted not only the poet and
story-teller, but the musician and the choreographer, too. *Swan Lake*
is the earliest of the Tchaikovsky ballets, and by many the best loved.
The dreamy magic of motion and music well matches the pensive
story ; the preening movements and bird-like poses of the dancers
suggest the grace of the swan, and the illusion is enhanced by the white
ballet skirt and pale pink shoes. The curtain rises ; we see a crowned
swan swimming across the lake, and we share the emotion of the
prince, fated to wed an unknown bride, and vaguely aware of the love
for which his heart is waiting. His thoughts turn confusedly, we may
guess, to swans and the swan-maidens of whom he has dreamed. His

expectations are fulfilled when Odette, the swan-princess, appears, an enchanted maiden compelled by magic to take this form, regaining her human shape only at this destined hour. Her companion swan-maidens gather as the prince and princess walk together in the wood. Huntsmen threaten to shoot the birds, but the prince returns in time to stop them. And now they dance together as she rejoins him from the wood. Flocks of swans and cygnets come to share in the dance, and the princess lets the prince know that if a man should love her and marry her the spell of enchantment will be broken. He vows his love ; he will choose her for his bride at the ball. But the magician, who has enchanted the swans, tricks him by causing his daughter to assume Odette's appearance. The prince chooses the sorcerer's daughter, and so breaks his vow ; and we see Odette at the window in a heartbreaking scene in which she watches the dance and vainly tries to warn him. Here the story has taken a different turn from that of the usual swan-maiden drama, but much of the traditional legend has been preserved.

A curious feature of the swan-maiden legend—and it appears in other folk-tales about enchanted damsels and spellbound wives—is that the husband may not ask his consort's name if he wishes to keep her. This is an instance of a widespread belief in the danger of communicating to another so personal a possession as one's name. To the primitive mind a name is thought to be part of its owner, and one puts oneself in the power of the man who learns it.

As with the wife, so with the husband. This is illustrated by the medieval romance of the Knight of the Swan, which has persisted through the ages in various forms. Perhaps the earliest, an old French tale, is that of Helias, the legendary ancestor of the dukes of Brabant and of the celebrated Godfrey of Bouillon, the first king of Jerusalem. Beatrice, married to the son of Queen Matabrune, bears him seven children, six sons and a daughter, each with a silver collar round its neck. The wicked queen seeks to destroy the children, but her plots only succeed in depriving them of their collars. By this they are changed into swans, all but Helias the youngest, who escapes because he has been adopted by a hermit. He vows to restore his brothers and sister to their human shape. He is successful with five of them, but one remains a swan, his collar having been melted down to make a drinking-cup for Matabrune. Helias now embarks in a boat drawn by his swan-brother, and comes to champion the princess who claims the duchy of Bouillon. He is victorious ; he marries her, but warns her not to ask his name. She, however, disobeys, whereupon the swan reappears with his boat and Helias sails away.

Grimm has adapted part of this story in his tale, 'The White Bride and the Black Bride.' Here the mother and the stepsister push the true bride into the water, where she is immediately turned into a snow-white swan. The legend also is the source of the well-known tale of Lohengrin and Elsa, of which there are various versions. Elsa, in prison on the false charge of doing away with her brother, the heir to the duchy, longing for a champion, remembers that she can summon him by ringing the little bell which a falcon has brought to her from the sky. The bell is a manifestation of that which guards the Holy Grail, of which Lohengrin's father, Parzifal, is the keeper. Lohengrin, who has been chosen to defend an innocent person, has been carried away from the Castle of the Grail in a little boat drawn by a snow-white swan, and reminded that a servant of the Grail must not reveal his name unless asked to do so, and that once he has made himself known he must return to the holy mountain. So when Elsa calls him by ringing her bell he comes in his swan-boat and proves himself her champion in the lists. They marry, but, alas ! Elsa, provoked by malicious whispers, asks the knight's name, and Lohengrin, having declared himself, summonses with his magic horn the swan which comes to the sound of the faint music, and the boat bears him away, but not before the missing prince, changed by enchantment into the swan, has resumed his human form.

In the sober annals of history the swan has played almost as distinguished a part as in the fairyland of folklore. In England the swan is, and has been for centuries, a royal bird. It was the property of the king and of those nobles, monasteries, boroughs and country gentlemen to whom the king granted the special privilege of keeping swans. The very names, 'swan' and 'cygnet,' indicate the bird's place in social history. Just as the Saxon churl in *Ivanhoe* points out that humble British pig, ox, and calf become aristocratic Norman pork, beef and veal when dressed for the alien lord's table, so does the English swan turn into the French cygnet. Swan's flesh was always considered a great delicacy. I understand that cygnets are still fattened for the table at the swanpit in Norwich.

It is in the Fens and surrounding districts that the first reference to the keeping of swans in captivity occurs, and where the earliest code of swan law belongs. There is evidence that within a hundred years of the Norman Conquest swans were kept at Stowe in Norfolk. We find Henry III asking the prior of Spalding and the abbot of Croyland to provide swans for the royal table. For the king's Christmas at York no less than 125 were ordered, together with vast numbers of hens, partridges, cranes, peacocks, pheasants, rabbits and hares.

In the centuries that follow we find many references to the king's prerogative where swans are concerned—his 'game' of swans—and to private owners, who were gradually coming to include people of lesser social standing. But it remained the law that all swans at liberty in open or common waters belonged to the Crown. A subject could keep them on his moat or private waters : to keep them on open or common waters he had to have a licence.

It is not surprising, therefore, that rules defining the king's privileges, and governing the preservation and registration of the birds, were evolved and gradually codified. The earliest detailed regulations that we have are those drawn up for the Lincolnshire river Witham in Henry VIII's reign. With this document, which came into the possession of Sir Joseph Banks and passed from him to the Royal Society, is an elaborate roll of illustrations of 'swan marks.' Such were necessary to identify the swans and cygnets of the different owners. The marks were patterns or nicks cut into the bird's bill. Though it might seem impossible to devise so many varied marks in so limited a space there were over five hundred marks for the Lincolnshire area alone.

Swan marks usually descended from father to son, and could be left by will. In some cases the mark was attached to a particular manor and passed from owner to owner. Others belonged to corporate towns, religious houses, guilds and villages, even to the parish church. They could be bought and sold ; sometimes they were leased.

Every year an expedition was planned by the Royal Swanmaster, to 'take up' or mark the cygnets bred in his district since his previous visit. This ceremony was, in consequence known as 'swan-upping.' Both the ritual and the term survive to this day, though 'swan-upping' is now confined to the Thames, on which the Crown and the two London companies of Vintners and Dyers own the swans. The ceremony takes place on the last Monday in July, when the cygnets are about two months old. The three swanmasters meet together at Southwark Bridge, and proceed on the 'swan-voyage.' The Vintners' Company is said to possess in some years as many as five hundred swans. Its mark, consisting of two nicks, is believed to be the origin of the inn sign 'The Swan with Two Necks,' a corruption of the correct title.

Though the picturesque records of the swan-masters show that an encouraging swan population lives today on the Thames, there seems little doubt that in the great fen areas and other places where the bird once abounded the numbers have sadly declined. We must turn to Abbotsbury in Dorset to see the swan in his pristine opulence. Here is the famous swannery where, owing to the nice admixture of the waters of the sea and the river Fleet, swans have established themselves since the dawn of history. On a level spit of land under Chapel Hill, cut off from the sea by the Chesil Beach, is an immense sanctuary of more than a thousand swans. Standing among the reeds or floating on the blue waters, their astonishing snow-whiteness, grace and aloofness are enough to account for all the legends of regal enchantment that have accompanied them down the centuries.

From the lithograph by John James Audubon

[211]

THE MYSTERY OF
THE GLASTONBURY THORN

by MILES HADFIELD

 F THE OAK stubbornly and sturdily symbolizes the practical genius of the English, the hawthorn surely suggests the magic of English poetry. No other tree, except perhaps the yew, is so nobly endowed with mystery. Not even our own hygienic age has succeeded in sterilizing the necromancy which lingers among the dense tangle of branches.

Over much of England, in the south-west of Scotland, in the Isle of Man, and particularly in Ireland, there still lingers a superstition that ill-luck follows when hawthorn flowers are cut. In parts of Devon, for example, old people still remember hawthorn as 'death-flower.' And there are several ancient legends, such as that describing the chapter of disasters befalling Tim MacDougal when he felled a thorn for money, all boding evil to those who damage the tree. A number of old thorns, such as the Witch of Hethel, near Norwich, are known to have been maintained for centuries. Quite often a legend associates misfortune with those who have damaged them.

One of these ancient trees was inherited by Dr. Vaughan Cornish, who made a detailed study of the historic thorn trees of England. He collected local records of thorn-lore and superstition. He mapped all the places and districts (such as the 'hundreds') which take their names from thorns. Combining the two, he found that places and legends came from comparatively well defined areas. There was a band running from Dorset across to Middlesex, with an offshoot up the Wye valley, but not reaching Wales. Another patch included Hertfordshire and Essex, with a branch running up to Cambridge and Norwich, where it suddenly ended. Parts of Yorkshire had the thorn cult too, as did the Isle of Man and the Solway Firth. It was powerful above all throughout Ireland.

He soon interpreted the significance of this geography. The cult of the thorn—with comparable legends—exists also in parts of France. The areas in England which show the cult are precisely those known to have been colonized before and immediately after the first Roman occupation by the same tribes coming from the parts of France where the thorn cult still remains. Thus the sudden ending of the cult at Norwich is explained because the Belgae, who fostered it, here came up against the hostile Icenii, who did not.

Ireland was colonized direct by people of a similar tribe, who only made contact with England by using the Isle of Man as a port of call, and who have left no traces in Anglesey.

That, then, is an explanation of the localization of our thorn cult—though, of course, with the passage of time the superstitions have overflowed somewhat beyond their original bounds.

What was the original cult of the thorn? Anthropologists today wisely insist that no cult or religion has an entirely rationalistic basis, but there is no doubt that it was closely connected with the use of thorn trees as landmarks, meeting places, or as sites for mystical rites. We must remember that hawthorn is a tree growing away from woodland, often in featureless, open places, and that old trees develop singular and easily recognized shapes. What could be better as a signpost or boundary-mark ? And is it not likely that the officials, then as now, would weave a lot of mumbo-jumbo around anything whose protection was vital to the community ?

The most famous relic of our thorn cult, and one that gets into our newspapers most years, is the Christmas-flowering Glastonbury thorn.

When Joseph of Arimathaea came to this country, bringing with him the Christian faith, he landed on the Isle of Avalon—famed in the Arthurian legend. The old man, fatigued with the climb up a steep hill, and, no doubt, enervated by the trying prospect of converting us, plunged his staff into the ground. The day was Christmas Eve. Suddenly, a most heartening miracle took place. The staff, which was of hawthorn, broke into leaf and flower. It was a sign of encouragement to Joseph, and to all those who beheld it, of the miraculous power of his faith. When Glastonbury Abbey was built nearby, the thorn, now rooted, was transferred within its precincts. Those who have subsequently tried to destroy the tree have met with most unpleasant consequences.

Now let us follow the history of the tree and its legend a little more closely. First, we should say that Avalon was, in fact, the largest of a series of small islands surrounded by swamp and water which until comparatively modern times occupied the district where Glastonbury stands ; Wearyall Hill still exists.

Dean Armitage Robinson, the great authority on Glastonbury, has unearthed the first record of the thorn, which 'do burge and bere greene leaves at Christmas' and 'groweth in Werall.' This was written about 1502.

In 1613 Michael Drayton writes of the 'three times famous Ile' of Glastonbury—famed for 'great Arthur's tomb,' 'holy Joseph's grave,' and where 'trees yet in winter bloome, and bear their Summer's green.' Not until 1635, with the visit of Sir William Brereton (later to become a famous Parliamentary general), do we get a full and first-hand account of the tree, 'so famous and so much visited and frequented on the day of Christ's nativity.' It then grew half a mile from Glastonbury, on the right-hand side of the road to Bridgwater.

Sir William collected branches and leaves, and carved his initials on the trunk—at the same time observing that it was in a bad way owing to his many predecessors who had done the like. He censures the local inhabitants for not taking proper care of it. A number of grafts had at divers times been taken, one forming a notable tree at a tavern near the George ('whereof also I brought away with me some branches'). He was assured by many, however, that with the exception of the tree by the George, the grafted trees 'degenerate from their much to be admired budding and blossoming.'

In the same year, Lt. Hammond of Norwich, who had wearied himself 'tossing and tumbling their saints bones,' inspected the thorn, and also the one at the tavern, which, after a 'glasse of good sacke,' he reported as 'springing and flourishing' when he passed on his way.

About the same time we hear something of the dire effects of cutting the holy tree. It is true that James Howell was strongly biased against the enemies of Petropolis—as he called the Puritans—and his odd book, *Dodona's Grove, or the Vocall Forest*, is political rather than scientific. Howell considers that 'he was well served of his blind zeal, who going to cut down an ancient white hawthorn-tree, which because she budded before others, might be an occasion of superstition, had some of the prickles flew into his eye, and made him monocular.' Thus the thorn cult legend crops up again during the reign of Charles I.

Let us now turn to the scientists. John Parkinson in 1640 refers to '*Spina acuta biflora Britanica*, England's Hawthorn.' He tells us that this 'grows in divers places in our land, where it is not greatly wondered at by those who live there.' He names trees at Glastonbury Abbey, at High St. or Whey St. in Romney Marsh, and near Nantwich in Cheshire. (That reliable botanist, John Goodyer, had reported the Whey St. tree in 1605.)

In 1646 Sir Thomas Browne was even more outspoken. He points out that precociousness is known in many trees other than the 'Glassenbury' thorn, and 'strange effects are naturally taken for miracles by weaker heads.' He adds 'such a thorn there is in Parham Park, Suffolk and elsewhere.'

That industrious early Victorian, Agnes Strickland, unearthed in France an account of a Christmas spent at the court of Charles II by Père Cyprian Gamache in 1660. Christmas, he tells us, is always celebrated in England with greater pomp than in any other European realm. Flowers of the Glastonbury thorn, which usually flowers on Christmas Eve, are brought up in procession on Christmas morning and presented to the King and Queen. This thorn, he says, was much venerated by the English, who told him that St Joseph of Arimathaea brought to Glastonbury a thorn out of our Lord's Crown, and placed it in the earth. Thenceforth it blossomed on Christmas Day. He adds a joke made by Charles I, who, when presented with the thorn, was told that its flowering was much venerated by English Catholics. 'Why so?' said the king. 'You bring me this miraculous thorn blooming on Christmas Day Old Style; the Pope and your thorn differ not a little, for he celebrates Christmas ten days earlier by the style of the New Calendar than we do.'

This is, I believe, the first recorded account connecting Joseph with the origin of the thorn ; it is entirely omitted from those other authors whom I have quoted. By some authorities the origin of this part of the legend is attributed to an eighteenth-century descendant of the keeper of the inn mentioned by Sir William Brereton.

Great interest was aroused in 1723 when belatedly the New Style calendar was introduced to us from the Continent. Unaware of Charles I's previous observations, a large crowd attended Glastonbury on the new Christmas Day. The thorn did not flower, but on the old Christmas Day (now January 6) it was in full bloom ! So much for these new-fangled ideas, they said.

In more recent times, the most interesting development is the manner in which this cult, while still maintained at Glastonbury, has spread to Herefordshire. In the nineteenth century there appear to have been no less than eleven hawthorn trees in that county which were venerated. Today, practically each New Year every one of several still remaining gets a visit from a journalist and its photograph in the papers. There are, of course, offspring from the original Glastonbury tree growing in botanical and private gardens, but some at least of the Herefordshire trees are in quite remote places and it is improbable that all of them derive from Glastonbury.

But now the time has come to see what our patient scientists and researchers of the present century have to tell us.

The Isle of Avalon, they assure us, we can accept. As the largest of a group of islands, it was a much used landing place, and some ancient thorn was its landmark and site for meeting. Undoubtedly heathen magic would be used to protect it. When Christianity came, the Church would naturally take it over, and endow it with Christian attributes. Was the original landmark a precocious flowering tree, or did the monks find one, and, from its flowering at about the time of the Nativity, might they not more easily be able to transfer the allegiance of the common people from the heathen mark thorn to the new Christian miraculous thorn—a new mystery more potent than the old ?

And of Joseph of Arimathaea—and for that matter, King Arthur and the Holy Grail ? In the early twelfth century a very complete account was written of the antiquities of Glastonbury. A few years later Geoffrey of Monmouth fully wrote of the Arthurian legends. The first mentions neither Joseph nor Arthur, the second has no reference to Glastonbury.

In 1184 the Abbey was burned down. The Abbot launched an appeal for funds to rebuild it. As we should say today, the response fell far short of the target. And, following this failure (it is sad to relate), stories of the connection with the Abbey of Arthur and Guinevere and Joseph of Arimathaea began to circulate. (The romance of Arthur and his knights was then all the rage.) One imagines that the Abbot smiled as the flow of pilgrims steadily increased and his building fund grew.

Now about the thorn. Botanically, it is *Crataegus monogyna biflora*. Parkinson, you will note, used the name *biflora*. It is a form of the common hawthorn that produces two batches of flower buds. The first can be seen developing in autumn. They are usually ready to open at about Christmas time, particularly if a few mild days occur (not unusual at that season—and some say that the tree flowers less regularly now in the cold light of electric torches than it did when scrutinized under the warm glow of a hundred lanterns). In spring, *biflora* produces another crop of normal flowers. This phenomenon is also found in other trees. There is, for instance, a flowering cherry, Jugatsu Sakura (*Prunus subhirtella autumnalis*) from Japan, now quite often seen in our gardens. It usually blooms rather earlier than the Glastonbury thorn, and far outdoes our native phenomenon in beauty.

So now we know all—disillusion is complete. A botanical sport, a bit of smart work to convert the heathens, a publicity stunt. . . . But I wonder. Have you ever seen a tree of this famous thorn growing truly wild ? I never have, nor can I read of one. Is there not after all something mysterious and rather wonderful left ? The puritan who lopped the tree became monocular ; may not we, too, who have not only lopped the legend but rooted it up, be in danger of losing half our light as well ?

TREASURES OF THE GRAMOPHONE

by PHILIP HOPE-WALLACE

HERE OUGHT TO BE a word, and no doubt the Germans have a word, for unserious collectors of just-vanished experiences. 'Collector' will not do at all. I strongly repudiate the idea of myself as a collector, except in the involuntary sense of accumulating collars of a size one can no longer wear. I abhor collectors in general ; they conjure up a generic image of a bore in a green eyeshade poring over Penny Blacks, or is it Cabbage Whites ?—Worse, reaching you down from the top shelf Sarah's very own copy of *Zaza*.

Yet just such a bore I dare say I shall become. For this habit of wanting to capture the recent past will in the end bury me under a shoal of old soup-plate-like gramophone records, to say nothing of albums of cuttings, 'stills' and old photographs, especially those of dead *divas*, the sort whose manifold chins are veiled in rolled coils of pearls, the topmost strand of these held enticingly near the lips like one about to eat corn on the cob.

'Fancier' is the word, not collector. A collector collects seriously. I only like what springs my imagination, not necessarily what is rare.

And I must confess that this applies as much to films as to ancient vocal discs : in fact the fascination is the same. I would barter you a record of Christabel Pankhurst's 'Rush the House of Commons' speech for that strip of film, duration not more than thirty seconds, wherein you see the Countess Tolstoy exacerbating the patience of her great old man by trying to stick a buttonhole in his lapel on his way down the garden at Yasna Polyanna. Or perhaps better, the last Czarina, in a hat like the *howdah* on an elephant, opening a bazaar, or Cléo de Mérode doing an Egyptian dance, or that early Desdemona, the late Lillian Nordica, kicking off at a Chicago policeman's football match in a hobble skirt and a muff which touches the ground.

Such things, it may be said very reasonably, are in every other library of notable films ; London, Moscow, New York can all display such treasures. The newly opened Cinemathèque in Paris contains gems richer than those listed above. Similarly, for a few extra pounds you can recover from the makers or from those specialist clubs which exploit the fairly common addiction to which I plead guilty, hundreds of 'historic' discs. Perhaps one should look at it the other way (sure sign of collector's madness) and demand to know why *everyone* is not struck paralytic with excitement to see Tolstoy strut and grumble, or to hear Alfred, Lord Tennyson, thunder out a few lines of *The Charge of the Light Brigade*. And have you heard Gladstone ? Who can truly say he knows anything of the history of England who has not heard with his own ears the ringing unction in *that* voice ?

I cannot see that this is unreasonable. There is a very famous early snippet of film, end of the last century perhaps, or at any rate earlier than the Queen Victoria Funeral pictures, with Kaiser Bill on horse-back, wherein one sees a horse-drawn fire-engine responding to a call. At one moment a bulky matron holding up her skirts from the mud darts into the picture, shoots us a baleful look and withdraws. Who, ah, who is she ? My fancy will not let her alone : was she the cameraman's mother, a jealous sweetheart ; perhaps, merely curious ? Every time I see this fragment, this woman, now dead I must suppose, grows in my imagination till she has a stature exceeding most of the figures of history or fiction. I have lately rather come to believe that she was running away from some horrid husband in one of Mr Arnold Bennett's books but that she couldn't resist the lure of the fire-engine bell and came to look. Well, there she is ; as far as I am concerned as permanent a part of history as Proust's Odette or Frances Cornford's Fat White Woman whom nobody loved, gloved amid the happy summer fields. Long may she dart !

A true collector of the treasures of the gramophone will assail you briskly with a jargon about processes which I find infinitely tedious. I am, of course, grateful for the detective work which these unflinching searchers apply to the precise dating of early discs. Talk of 'Hill and Dale' recording, 'pre-Dogs' and such, sounds sweet enough in my ear, but largely incomprehensible. Light-heartedly I like the rewards without the toil, the fun without the bookwork. The loss no doubt is mine. But I say I come to it with an undulled ear. I cannot, for instance, tell you how many years separate the cylinder recordings (about half a minute in length) which Colonel Mapleson made in the 'flies' of the New York Metropolitan Opera House during an all-star *Huguenots* in 1901, and the gramophone records of Arditi's 'Se saran rose' by the same great *diva* recording somewhere in London rather late (one guesses) on a morning when things had not been going too smoothly for the quick-natured Australian singer. Perhaps (if I were a professional collector I should try to find out) they had had to remake the innocent little waltz song many times over ; at any rate, what is captured on wax is sung with such a concentration of fury as would shrivel any roses which might survive from the title. If Melba were older when this last was made and the cares of the world were reflected in her voice, at least the recording was less noisy than on the old Mapleson cylinders. Yet these, too, have an excitement all their own : if only because you unquestionably do hear a wholly different sort of Melba, with a youthfulness and dazzling clarity of voice. A 'live' occasion—what a difference it makes. It is the volume and realism of applause which in this case (through the 'frying' and scratching of the surface) assure you that the voice in fact at that date was *like* that. Strange, to re-live that long-dead minute when the new soprano out in the New World made a 'new' society audience at the Met. cheer for her. One has read countless descriptions of such occasions—*divas* are not a race to let them slip into oblivion ; one has seen such scenes laboriously reconstructed in fictional or biographical films. Yet a snippet of the real thing—how vastly much more it tells you.

The essence of the sought-after thrill is the recapturing across a space of time of an experience or performance which in its own time was *consuming time*. I do not derive commensurable interest from gazing at old photographs (frozen seconds), rather sharing Proust's opinion that nothing so kills our remembrance of how people looked as the photograph which shows you indeed how—in the fullest detail. I derive practically no thrill at all from toying with Flaubert's pencil or having in my hands or on my feet Hans Andersen's galoshes. I am not quick to people deserted palaces with defunct and suffering monarchs ; for me no Moberley and Jourdain experience of the mistress of the Little Trianon. But a gramophone record of Sarah Bernhardt, a snippet of Pavlova dancing—one learns with extra interest : during the lunch hour when the studio attendants were not there to spy on her—such things carry me into the past with the ease and speed of H. G. Wells's time machine pressed to the fullest throttle.

I am quite prepared to be told that this is merely a matter of being in one's forties. It may well be that I belong to a uniquely placed generation. One's father, or father's father, saw nothing special in such relics, for they were merely copies of something they had themselves experienced directly. A later generation than mine, used to the social agony of having its earliest baby lispings played back at it at all ages from the family tape-recorder, will see no magic, but merely catalogue value, in either discs or films of a vanished past. Besides the extreme smoothness, the sheer ease of recording or re-creating the sounds of the past strangely lessen the excitement of submission to the ritual.

When one used to put one's head half-way inside a horn suspended from the ceiling by an indestructible pulley fitment, and the voice of the past was preceded and accompanied by a noise like a thousand trains in tunnels and all the roaring of the seven seas, then indeed did one crouch in awe as before a Delphic oracle.

If they were hard to hear, those early ones, how much harder—the evidence was joyously imprinted on many of them—must they have been to make. Not Pachman only muttered to himself. One knows other treasures where a warning cry of 'Look out !' preludes some would-be 'off-hand' ballad piece, or a triumphant 'Howzatt ?' all too speedily rounds off a soulful monologue. The missed entry, the bosh-shot *cadenza*, the swear-word hastily bitten off—these and a thousand other treasured blemishes were allowed out to the world in the old days. Nowadays we have to content ourselves with Toscanini bursting into song *pour encourager les autres* or an occasional shout from the touchline by Beecham : thinner days, ours.

Connoisseurship is not enough. One gets to know one's own records too well. It becomes as simple, and sometimes actually more rewarding, to *remember* how John McCormack produces a perfect diminuendo at the climax of Liza Lehman's 'Ah, Moon of My Delight' than to rout the faintly warped old disc from its lair and perform it. So showmanship enters the field. One needs a stranger, a victim, a target for one's records. Sometimes, having snared one, it becomes evident that he is only *pretending* to appreciate the pearls you strew before him, the swine. At such times, I feel I understand the deep sadness of elderly millionaires who would give anything to be loved or to wolf down a Châteaubriand steak—and digest it.

There is a much-loved B.B.C. programme called 'Desert Island Discs' in which, with varying degree of bogus *bonhomie*, celebrities tell us of the gramophone records they would take with them for a long sequestration. The choices are often frivolous ; seldom, if ever, showing real thought. Some would induce madness quickly enough. A much better game, if you have any sort of a collection yourself, is to ask yourself which half-dozen discs you would snatch from a hypothetical fire in your cupboard. And this will also tell you which sort of a collector you are : an amateur of the game ; or a speculator. If the latter, your choice would no doubt go to the pre-1904 Fonotypias or whatever stands highest in the collector's market at the moment. But if you are a historian you might well feel that antiquity in itself was all that mattered, and seize up, alone and precious, *Dan Leno : 'Going to the Races.'* But your real lover of the voice from the past will have his work cut out to make a fast selection today, when even Yvonne Printemps and Elisabeth Schumann have vanished from the lists. I know that I should have to salvage my Alma Glucks and McCormacks, some old Sembrichs, as thick-edged as Crown Derby saucers, an old and far-off Russian nightingale or two, Caruso singing the recruiting song 'Over there' (second verse in French *Par là-bas*) and perhaps *Lord Avebury, 'A speech to the boys'* (1906) as well. But imagination, collector's mania and truth all merge together here. I see myself in night attire, flames at my back, heedless of danger while my finger runs happily o'er the lists. What about 'Whistling and comic monologues' and 'Three minute sermons ?' or Lewis Waller's 'Once more into the breach' and *Amy Johnson : My impressions of my Flight.* And, of course, Alfred Lester's *The Meanderings of Monty.* It would be a pleasant death.

THE REBUS

by DEREK HUDSON

T HE REBUS, deriving from the Latin 'by things,' is familiar to us nowadays as a puzzle-letter or tale in children's papers. Its history has been long and obscure. The hieroglyphic writing of the ancient Egyptians, which persisted until the fourth century A.D., embodied the idea of representing words by pictures, though only as part of a highly complicated system of its own. The same idea occurs in heraldry and in certain devices or pictorial signatures which were popular in the Middle Ages. In the roof of the Islip chapel in Westminster Abbey, the Abbot's name is depicted (among other ways) by a man falling from a tree and, presumably, crying 'I slip.' William Camden (1551–1625), the antiquary, records that a love-sick rustic painted on the border of his gown a rose, a hill, an eye, a loaf, and a well : 'Rose Hill I love well.' Such enigmas early attracted the ingenious minds of the French. Gilles Ménage, the seventeenth-century scholar, derived the rebus from satirical pieces composed by clerks in Picardy for the annual carnival, topical hits, in fact, which were entitled *de rebus quae geruntur*, 'about things which are going on.'

The following pages contain examples of the rebus letter in four centuries, together with some tentative interpretations. The earliest example that I have been able to find is that which Princess Louise, daughter of Elizabeth, Queen of Bohemia, and a sister of Prince Rupert, addressed 'For the Ld Goring' on a certain January 4 from The Hague, where the Queen held her exiled court. The most likely period for its composition is 1647–50. Lord Goring was then about forty, a handsome, dashing, but dangerously unreliable royalist commander in the Civil War, who had suffered his final defeat at Langport in 1645 ; he went to Holland in 1646 in command of the English regiments in Spanish service, and to Spain in 1650. Louise would have been in her twenties, a talented artist and a lively, amiable girl—Bohemian in more senses than one. That she was fond of Goring seems likely from the great pains she took over this letter, which she concludes 'Your loving sister.' Goring died in 1657, and in 1658—perhaps a pure coincidence

—Louise retired into a Catholic convent. She lived until 1709, enjoying a cheerful old age as Abbess of Maubuisson.

Princess Louise's delightful letter shows the rebus being used, as in the case cited by Camden, to conceal an ignorance of language. Louise complains to Goring that, if only he had taught her how to write in English, as well as the use of the alphabet, she would have been able to produce a more intelligible letter (but N.B. I think she was also glad to be able to show off her drawing). By contrast, 'The Triumph of Liberty,' of 1765, by an unknown hand, partakes rather of the nature of a political 'Rébus de Picardie'—*de rebus quae geruntur*. John Wilkes was in Paris on February 14, 1765, when John Williams, a printer concerned in publishing No. 45 of *The North Briton*, was exposed in the pillory. The occasion, intended for the humiliation of Williams, was turned into an effective demonstration against Government. Jackboots were hung on ladders and a collection taken among the crowd realized £200 for Williams.

By the time that another century had lapsed the whimsical Victorians had adopted the rebus as the convenient vehicle for the amusement of the young that it remains to this day. The Rev. C. L. Dodgson, better known as Lewis Carroll, wrote his picture-letter to Ina Watson (one of three sisters, Harriet, Mary and Georgina, whom he addressed collectively as 'Harmarina') soon after he had moved his own sisters into a new family home at 'The Chestnuts,' Guildford. It dates, then, from 1869 or the early 1870's. The *genre* had changed little in the two hundred years since Princess Louise sat down to her task at The Hague. The very first sentence gives us the inevitable pictorial eye and the drawing of a post-letter which occur at the beginning both of Princess Louise's epistle and of the Wilkes broadsheet as well as the symbol of the deer which commences the latter. Students will observe the influence of Edward Lear on Lewis Carroll's draughtsmanship.

To the rebus, as to all his work, Rex Whistler brought a gay fluency and the wish to please. The letter published here was his charming way of thanking a friend of fifteen, Elizabeth Wellesley (now Lady Elizabeth Clyde) for a stay at Penns-in-the-Rocks in about 1935. The unlucky fall at the end of it brings us full circle to the Islip chapel. It must be emphasized that here, as in the other examples, the pictures are usually of objects whose names *sound* like the words. But practice is inconsistent. Spelling and aspirates go by the board. As in love, all's fair in the rebus.

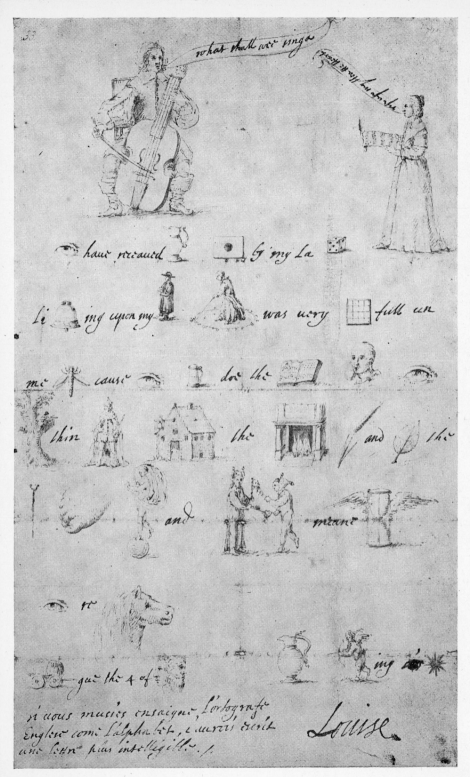

Letter from Princess Louise to Lord Goring, written between 1647 and 1650.
Transcription on p. 232. *By courtesy of the Trustees of the British Museum.*

The TRIUMPH of LIBERTY

A Hieroglyphical, Congratulatory Epistle

from John [Wilkes] Esq. to John [Williams] on the Applause

he Receiv'd at his Public Exhibition in Old Palace Yard, on Thursday Feb.ʳ 14.th being the 45.th day of the Year 1765.

My [rebus] Friend

'Tis [rebus] with the utmost Pleasure [rebus] Receiv'd [rebus] Agreable [rebus], the inward Satisfaction [rebus] felt on Reading the Contents, nothing could Equal [rebus] the Cause of LIBERTY and my [rebus] Country w[rebus] [rebus] Sways did [rebus] sh[rebus] espouse, nothing [rebus] g[rebus]ve me such [rebus]nexpressive joy, [rebus] hea[rebus] there are [rebus] some Advocates for the good Old Cause, and [rebus] Sp[rebus]te of Scottish pr[rebus]de or [rebus] Power, the Liberty of the Press so very [rebus] my Fellow Country [rebus] tot[rebus]y abol[rebus]sd; a Pr[rebus]vilege [rebus] English[rebus] [rebus] Boasted of super[rebus] our [rebus] other Nat[rebus]ons. [rebus] [rebus]ly Congratulate [rebus] on the Success [rebus]ve hither[rebus] met with, and S[rebus]ncerely n[rebus]sh [rebus]t may Cont[rebus]nue [rebus] [rebus] doubt [rebus], [rebus] know[rebus]ng the Honest [rebus] of my Country[rebus] who are [rebus] ready [rebus] protect y[rebus] [rebus]njured and oppose the Comb[rebus]nat[rebus]ons of Weak or Wicked [rebus] of State, an ev[rebus]dent proof of [rebus] w[rebus] shown by the [rebus]r Behav[rebus]our [rebus]n Palace Yard where [rebus]m f[rebus]rmly persuaded had the Or[rebus]gin[rebus] Scotch [rebus] been he wou'd have Shared the same fate, b[rebus] the Un- -ani[rebus] Vo[rebus]ce of the [rebus]. Comfort [rebus]rself w[rebus]th these Reflect[rebus]ons and persevere [rebus]n the Cause of LIBERTY, for my own Part [rebus]m extremely happy [rebus]n [rebus]n Xile, Regretting noth[rebus]ng [rebus] the [rebus] Absence of my Fr[rebus]ends, and [rebus] hop[rebus]ng [rebus] see [rebus] w[rebus] Tranqu[rebus]llity sh[rebus] aga[rebus]n [rebus] Restored [rebus] m[rebus] [rebus] Nat[rebus]ve Country, and our Enem[rebus]es [rebus] promoted [rebus] a h[rebus]gher Stat[rebus]on, on Tower [rebus] and [rebus] and the whole Tr[rebus]be of Rebel Scotch [rebus] dr[rebus]ven [rebus] the[rebus] Northern Cl[rebus]mate, the other side the Tweed.

[rebus]'am S.ⁱʳ [rebus]r Sincere [rebus] W[rebus]sher

I. WILKS. 1765.

The [snowballs]

My [deer] Ina,

    Though [eye] don't give birthday presents, still [eye] April ... write a birthday [letter] June [eye] came 2 your [door] 2 wish U many happy returns of the day, [barrel] the [cat] met me, [hand] took me for a [snake], [hand] hunted me [hand] and [hand] till [foot] could hardly [well] However somehow [eye] got into the [house], [hand] there a [snake] met me, [hand] took me for a [animal], and pelted me

Letter from Lewis Carroll (the Rev. C. L. Dodgson) to Ina Watson with   ,   ,

        . Of course   ran
into the street again,   a
        met me   took me
for a   ,   dragged me
all the way 2 the   ,
        the worst of all was when
a   met me   took
me for a   . I was
harnessed 2 it,   had
2 draw it miles and miles,
all the way 2 Merrow. So
U C I couldn't get 2 the
room where U were.
        However I was glad to

hear U were hard at work
learning the [multiplication table grid] for a
birthday treat.

I had just time 2 look
into the kitchen, and 
your birthday feast
getting ready, a nice 
[dish drawing] of crusts, bones, pills,
cotton-bobbins, and rhubarb
and magnesia— "Now," I
thought, "she will be happy!"
and with a [face drawing] I went
on my way—
Your aff^te friend
[signature]

By courtesy of Messrs Macmillan & Company

Letter from Rex Whistler to Elizabeth Wellesley (Lady Elizabeth Clyde)

TRANSCRIPTIONS OF THE REBUSES

LETTER FROM PRINCESS LOUISE TO LORD GORING

I have receaved your letter by my Ladies libelling upon my teacher (?) which was very painful to me because I can doe the music when I am thinking in the fireplace here and leave the Pintos (?) globe-trotters and Jesters meantime I remain your loving sister, Louise.
Hague the 4 of January
If you had taught me the English writing as you did the alphabet, I should have written a more intelligible letter.

LETTER FROM JOHN WILKES TO JOHN WILLIAMS

My dear Friend, 'Twas with the utmost Pleasure I Receiv'd your Agreable letter, the inward satisfaction I felt on Reading the Contents, nothing could Equal, as the Cause of LIBERTY and my dear Country was what I always did & ever shall espouse, nothing can give me such inexpressive joy, as hearing there are still some Advocates for the good Old Cause, and that in spite of Scottish pride or Episcopal Power, the Liberty of the Press so very dear to my Fellow Countrymen can not be totally abolished ; a Privilege that Englishmen ever Boasted of superior to all other Nations. I heartily Congratulate you on the success you've hitherto met with, and sincerely wish it may Continue which I doubt not, well knowing the Honest hearts of my Countrymen who are ever ready to protect ye Injured and oppose the Combinations of Weak or Wicked Men of State, an evident proof of which was shown by their Behaviour in Palace Yard where I'm firmly persuaded had the Original Scotch Jackboot been he wou'd have shared the same fate, by the Unanimous Voice of the People. Comfort yourself with these Reflections and persevere in the Cause of LIBERTY, for my own Part I'm extremely happy even in Exile, Regretting nothing but the Absence of my Friends, and still hoping to see ye Time when Tranquillity shall again be Restored to my dear Native Country, and our Enemies be promoted to a higher Station, on Tower Hill and . . (?) . and the whole Tribe of Rebel Scotch be driven to their Northern Climate, the other side the Tweed.
I am Sir your sincere Well wisher,
J. WILKS.

Readers are invited to decipher for themselves the letters from Lewis Carroll and Rex Whistler

SEASIDE REGENCY

drawn by PHILIP GOUGH

AS AN ILLUSTRATOR Philip Gough has always been very much at home in the Regency period. We discovered recently that one of his special interests is that elegant, classical, but distinctive architectural style which he calls 'Seaside Regency.' We persuaded him to let *Saturday Book* readers see some sketches from his note-books which, though architectural in aim, and closely related to existing buildings or documents of the period, are vivid reconstructions of Regency vistas as they must have appeared to Regency eyes. The view at the head of this page, for instance, reconstructed from an old print and from information gathered locally, shows Lyme Regis very much as Jane Austen must have seen it.

Sidmouth — The Esplanade

Weymouth

Worthing

Brighton

Scarborough — The Museum

Hastings — Pelham Crescent

The Saturday Book

CABINET

of

INVENTIONS

THE WARDIAN CASE

by KEN WILLIAMSON

URING THE SUMMER of 1829 a London doctor, Nathaniel
B. Ward, placed the chrysalis of a moth, a *Sphinx*,
in some moist earth contained in a wide-mouthed
bottle, covered with a lid. In watching the progress
of the moth from day to day he noticed that the
moisture which, during the heat of the day, arose
from the mould condensed on the glass and returned to the earth.
About a week before the final change of the insect, a seedling fern and a
grass made their appearance on the surface of the earth.

As a boy, Dr Ward had had an ambition to possess an old wall
covered with ferns and mosses. He had built up some brickwork at the
back of the house and placed a pipe at the top, from which water
trickled on the plants beneath. These were ferns and several mosses
procured from the woods in the neighbourhood of London, together
with primroses and wood sorrel. But owing to the effects of smoke
'issuing from surrounding manufactories' the plants soon began to
decline and ultimately they died.

To his delight, one of the ferns he had failed to cultivate in the
garden was now alive in the bottle. Its growth, he concluded, was due
to 'a moist atmosphere free from soot or other extraneous particles ;
light ; heat ; moisture ; periods of rest ; and change of air.'

Dr Ward concluded that all the conditions required for the growth of his ferns were fulfilled ; it remained for him to test the fact by experiment. He placed the bottle outside the window of his study and the plants continued to grow. They required no attention of any kind and remained in the bottle for nearly four years, until they accidentally perished. During his absence from home the rusting of the lid had allowed rain to enter the bottle. Long before this occurred, Dr Ward had carried out numerous experiments in closely-glazed cases which became known as Wardian Cases. In one of them, called the Tintern Abbey House, he placed a model of the west window of Tintern Abbey. The sides were built up with rock work to a height of about five feet and a perforated pipe passed around the top 'by means of which,' the doctor wrote 'I could rain upon the plants at pleasure.' There was no artificial heat and in the case were planted about fifty British, North American and other ferns. A double white camellia flowered for three successive years but was killed by the severity of the following winter. As he thought there would be insufficient light from any of his windows, Dr Ward placed a case of alpines on the roof of his

The Tintern Abbey House

home and all the plants flowered the following spring, excepting the andromedas. He allowed the plants to remain fully exposed to the sun for the whole year and some became exhausted and died ; but a few flowered in the following spring. No allowance had been made for the rest alpines have in winter when they are covered with snow. In his successive experiments he removed the case, after flowering, into the coldest and most shady place until the following season, when it was again placed in the sun. In this way the alpines flourished.

Two cases were filled with winter aconites and crocuses. One was placed outside a window with a southern aspect, where there was sufficient light, but no artificial heat ; the other in a warm room, where the light was very deficient. The plants in the former case exhibited a perfectly natural appearance and the flowers were abundant and well-coloured ; whilst in the latter the leaves were very long and pale, and not a single flower was produced.

Fairy roses were planted in a tub and covered with a bell-glass of rather smaller diameter than the tub. They flowered four or five months in every year, the only attention they required being a pruning after each flowering.

The largest experimental case was built in the doctor's house at Wellclose Square, Whitechapel. The length was twenty-four feet, width twelve, and the extreme height eleven feet. This house was heated in winter by means of hot-water pipes. In it were planted more than a hundred species of fern, some palms, two or three varieties of rose, numerous species of aloe, cactus and begonia, passion flowers and a fine collection of antediluvian plants. He placed a large earthen vessel containing twenty gallons of water, ten or twelve gold and silver fish and several aquatic plants in the centre of the case and the plants and fish continued to flourish for years.

It became obvious to Dr Ward that his method obviated all the difficulties of preserving plants during long sea voyages, and, in June, 1833, he filled two cases with ferns and grasses, and sent them to Sydney. The cases were refilled in Australia, and eight months later arrived in the English Channel. They were not watered once during the whole voyage and were 'in the most healthy and vigorous condition.' The Duke of Devonshire was one of the first to make use of the closed cases by sending one of his gardeners with them to the East Indies to procure some vegetable treasures for his conservatory at Chatsworth. A young Chinese or Cavendish banana plant was given by the Duke to a Mr Williams, who was about to leave England in 1839 for the Navigator Islands. In the following May it bore fruit and was eventually distributed in all parts of the islands, the Tongan Islands and the Fijis. No taller than six feet, the Chinese banana was not affected by winds as were the native bananas.

Robert Fortune, who was sent to China by the Horticultural Society, successfully brought back two hundred and fifteen out of two hundred and fifty plants in perfect health, whereas previously only one plant in a thousand survived the journey. Mr Fortune was sent to China by the

Honourable East India Company for the purpose of procuring tea plants for their possessions in the Himalayas. Twenty thousand tea plants were taken from Shanghai and introduced to the Himalayas. 'As to the cases themselves,' wrote Dr Ward in his book *On the Growth of Plants in Closely-Glazed Cases*, 'they admit of almost endless diversity of shape and size, from a wide-mouthed quart bottle to a building as large as the Crystal Palace, the larger indeed the better. It is always desirable to have an opening in the bottom as some plants are the better for occasional watering, and in the event of slugs getting into the mould, they may be destroyed by washing the earth with lime-water, which has thus a means of escape. Many cellular and flowerless plants will go on for a very long period without any fresh supply of water. I have now a bottle which was in the Exhibition, containing a fern or two with some mosses, which are in perfect health, and yet have not received any fresh water for eighteen years, and I believe it would be quite possible to fill a case with palms and ferns (placing it in a position where it would always obtain sufficient light and air) that would not require any water for fifty or a hundred years.'

The Wardian Case became the rage of the drawing-room. The bell-glasses, under which were kept wax, silk, and paper flowers, were used, and glaziers made cases to the instructions set out in Dr Ward's book. A Bristol glazier wrote to the doctor of 'the Lilliputian landscape' he had created by enclosing a space outside a window.

In a chapter in his book entitled 'On the Application of the "Closed" Plan in Improving the Condition of the Poor' Dr Ward suggested that primroses in early spring would repay the labour of fetching them, and would continue to flower for seven or eight weeks as sweetly as in their native woods. He also suggested cases of wood sorrel, the wood anemone, the yellow pimpernel, the veronica, the stitchwort, mosses and ferns. There were likewise many common garden plants procurable at little cost—lily of the valley, Solomon's seal, musk plant, myrtles, box, etc.—recommended

Plants in a Storage Bottle

for those with little light available. Where there was more sun, a greater number and variety of flowering plants would be found to thrive, including spring bulbs, crocuses, irises, hyacinths, narcissi, tulips, and passion flowers.

On retiring from his practice at Wellclose Square, Dr Ward went to live at Clapham Rise, where he was able to grow 'a much larger proportion of tropical plants than before.' He took the fish and plants from the large case in his old house and, with nothing to obstruct the rays of the sun, attempted to imitate in miniature a tropical forest. His new pool was larger and held about two hundred gallons of water.

In 1868 Dr Ward died at St Leonard's at the age of seventy-seven. In an appreciation written to a scientific journal, Dr J. D. Hooker said that without the aid of the Wardian Case a large proportion of the tropical plants cultivated in England could never have been introduced. He considered the doctor had afforded far greater and purer pleasures than all the artists, 'for a primrose placed in a bell-glass at Christmas in a London drawing-room will charm when a Raphael does not, and will charm none the less when a Raphael charms also.'

Nathaniel Ward had had an inclination for a seafaring life and his father, 'being aware of the realist mode of cure for such an inclination,' had sent him on a voyage to Jamaica when he was thirteen years old. The vessel in which he sailed was anchored off the island for some time, and Nathaniel spent his free time studying the natural history of the sea and shore. 'I never ceased admiring the various sea-birds, the Dolphin and the Flying Fish. My idle time was spent in sculling the jolly-boat to the edge of the coral reef and in ignorantly admiring the wondrous beauty of the vegetable and animal forms beneath.' This occupation was varied by an occasional excursion into the interior of the island. The tropical vegetation made an impression on his mind which was never effaced, and converted him into an ardent botanist. On his return to England, Ward seems to have been cured of his love for a sailor's life, and was soon apprenticed to the medical profession.

During the greater part of his life he was often out alone by sunrise in the summer time, at Shooter's Hill or Wimbledon, or elsewhere in the then open parts of London. He would make a collection of all the plants he could find and return home at the usual time to attend to his practice. About his house there was every possible contrivance for the growing of plants, but in the smoky atmosphere of the East End of London he was only able to maintain a fluctuating appearance of freshness by bringing back a renewed supply of plants on the occasion of any visit to a nursery or the country. Naturalists from all parts of the world frequented his home, where his many scientific friends flocked to see his plants and the many specimens and instruments he had collected to instruct and entertain them. A prominent feature of these gatherings was the microscope and its revelations.

The illustrations accompanying this article are of three Wardian cases, and wild plants which I have grown in a storage bottle. These consist of seedlings and ferns found growing in some moss in a garden. The bottom and sides of the bottle are lined with moss and aquarium gravel and pieces of charcoal sweeten the soil. Plants can be grown in this way in brandy glasses and bottles of all sizes and shapes. They provide, during the winter months, the spirit of the woods and, when the lid is lifted, the smell of spring.

In America, wild plants are grown in brandy-warmers, vinegar bottles, fish bowls, Mason jars, jelly glasses and old perfume bottles, and are called terrariums.

Although they are referred to in recent books on indoor gardening, published in this country, the actual Wardian Cases seem to have completely disappeared. Possibly the increasing interest in growing plants indoors will cause closed cases to be manufactured again, as they are being in America. Meanwhile, a search of your lumber-room might disclose some forgotten, but attractive, old bottle which would lend itself to a repetition of Dr Ward's experiments.

MOVING PICTURES
BEFORE THE CINEMATOGRAPH

by OLIVE COOK

E ARE APT to think of the cinema as having sprung into existence about fifty years ago as suddenly and as apparently mature as Euphorion ; or that, at the most, its ancestry can be no older than the invention of photography. But its history goes back as far as 1645, when Anasthasius Kircher made the first magic lantern ; and the stages which led to its birth are marked by innumerable pretty toys inspired by the discovery that the retina of the eye retains the impression of an object after its disappearance. Occasionally the evocative name of one of these toys, the Zoetrope, or perhaps the Praxinoscope, may figure in a sale catalogue ; but for the most part the enchanting contrivances based on the phenomenon of persistence of vision are not even names to us. The studio of the twin brothers John and William Barnes at Mousehole is probably the only place where they can still all be seen.

In that long, narrow room, are assembled not only the instruments which led directly to the development of cinematography, but countless other forms of optical illusion and animated pattern. Magic lanterns of all sizes and periods dominate the studio and call attention to the extensive library of exquisitely designed and painted slides.

Upon one of the tables lies a small round box. Though it might easily escape notice it is of great importance, for it contains the earliest practical application, in 1825, of persistence of vision. It is labelled 'Thaumatropical Amusement' and inside are a number of delicate little paper roundels, each with strings attached so that it may be twirled between fingers and thumbs. Each side of the disc presents a different image, but when it turns both images merge together. A bare tree puts on leaves, a bald man acquires a wig or a parrot enters his cage. The phenomenon was soon made to yield more spectacular results. When a circular design screwed to the top of an ivory handle is rotated opposite a looking-glass, a devil begins to turn somersaults or a blue bird flies round a rose bush. This is the Phenakistiscope.

But now Mr John Barnes is turning the slot-pierced drum of one of his Zoetropes. A long frieze has been placed inside the drum and as it revolves the slots reveal little figures leaping to life, a negro jumping through a hoop, a dolphin undulating through the waves. The effect is, however, so dazzling to the eye that it is impossible to look through the slots for more than a minute. In the Praxinoscope this disadvantage has been cleverly surmounted by abolishing the slots and placing mirrors in the centre of the drum to reflect and animate the circling images. The inventor improved even upon this by designing the charming Praxinoscope Theatre. Here the moving figures appear as if on a stage complete with painted proscenium. A child in a voluminous bathing costume swims with precise breast strokes in an ornamental lake or three boys play at leapfrog in a snowy landscape.

By the last decade of the nineteenth century the only moving images which had been projected were those produced by pulley, rackwork, rocking and lever lantern slides. A three-masted vessel would toss upon a sunlit ocean, a mill wheel would turn while the mill stream fell in a foaming cascade, or the chequered limbs of a harlequin would fly asunder. The isolated or jerky movement of these images was surpassed in 1890 when the Projecting Phenakistiscope was invented. By means of a single-blade shutter and a revolving disc the smoothly animated figures of blacksmiths working at an anvil or black boys diving into a pond would be flung upon the screen. But it was still not possible to project moving photographic pictures.

There already existed fat little books of photographs called Mutoscopes which sprang to life when flicked over by hand. And sometimes a mechanical device turned the pages as in the clockwork Kinora in the Barnes collection. By means of this wonderful instrument three persons at a time can watch a conjuror change a plate into a manikin or see horse-drawn traffic and pedestrians crossing Trafalgar Square in 1897. The Kinora is less poetic than the Praxinoscope Theatre but there is magic in the small scale of the moving picture. As soon as the invention of the film projector made it possible to enlarge the animated photographs and throw them on a screen much of the poetry vanished. The realism of the film relegated all the toys which had preceded it to the lumber room, to be remembered only by such collectors and enthusiasts as the brothers Barnes.

The photographs which follow were taken by Edwin Smith.

Above : the first film projector, patented in 1897 by Cecil Stafford Noble and Francis Liddell, used in combination with the magic lantern. *Below :* discs for the Zoetrope, *c.* 1868.

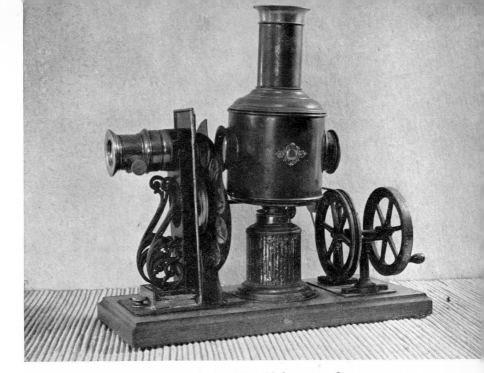

The Projecting Phenakistiscope, *c.* 1890.

Left : both sides of a Thaumatropic disc, *c.*
1826.   *Right :* a nineteenth-century French
magic lantern.   *Above :* a hand-painted slide
illustrating *Uncle Tom's Cabin*, *c.* 1850.
Below : hand-painted panoramic slide, *c.* 1820,
showing Napoleon's retreat from Moscow.

'Marianne Droz,' the automatic pianist, as she is today
Musée d'Histoire, Neuchâtel. *Photo. J. Erb*

THE MECHANICAL MUSICIANS

by JEREMY SANDFORD

Musikalische Zeitung, 1838

OLYMPIA PERFORMED with remarkable virtuosity on the piano and also sang a *bravura* air with a voice that was clear and ringing'—when Hoffmann used these words of the mechanical doll Olympia he was not describing a fantasy. Modern critics who congratulate operatic Olympias on their abrupt clockwork movements may not realize the perfection of the automata from which she was copied. Olympia was not unique. She was the product of an age fertile in life-sized mechanical musicians.

'On entering the salon,' wrote a correspondent in the *Musical Times* of a performance at the Paris Conservatoire, in 1838, 'I saw a well dressed, handsome figure of a man, apparently between forty and fifty, standing with a violin in his hand as if contemplating a piece of music which lay on a desk before him. . . . I had but little time for observation before the orchestra was filled by musicians, and on the leader taking his seat the figure instantly raised itself erect, bowed with much elegance two or three times, and then turning to the leader nodded as if to say that he was ready, and placed his violin to his shoulder. At the given signal he raised his bow, and applying it to the instrument produced *à la* Paganini one of the most thrilling and extraordinary flourishes I ever heard.'

The writer felt 'as if lifted from his seat,' and burst into tears, 'in which predicament were most persons in the room.' For the leader of the orchestra was not a human being but an automaton. The concert included 'a most beautiful fantasia in E natural,' a 'movement *allegro molto* on the fourth string solo which was perfectly indescribable,' and 'a cadenza, in which the harmonics double and single, arpeggios on the four strings, and saltos . . . were introduced with the greatest effect.' The author concludes 'I have heard the great Italian, I have heard the greater Norwegian, I have heard the best of music, but I never heard such sounds as then greeted my ear.'

Neither, judging by the illustration, had the orchestra. They are pictured gazing from behind their instruments, with the expressions usually reserved for conflagrations and Acts of God.

The 'great Italian' and 'greater Norwegian' referred to in the *Musical Times* are Paganini and Ole Bull, of which the former was at this date little short of a myth. An automaton considered superior to him can have been no mere musical toy ; and the Conservatoire, containing the most talented musicians in France, was not easily moved to tears.

Musical automata have a venerable ancestry. Archytas of Tarentum constructed a wooden pigeon which fluttered round the room and returned to his hand, Regiomantus an iron fly and an eagle which flew before the emperor Maximilian when he entered Nuremberg. Albertus Magnus employed an automaton doorkeeper which was destroyed by a pious friend, and Descartes an automatic young lady whom he kept in a box. Later, Friederich von Knauss constructed four speaking machines, of which the first was presented to Louis XV ; and in 1727 Pinchbeck of Haymarket devised 'an extraordinary piece of new machinery representing his sacred Majesty King George.'

Such, on one side, is the ancestry of Olympia. On the other she is descended from the numerous musical boxes and organs which were worked, like a modern musical box, on the barrel and pin principle. One of these was the miraculous organ sent by Queen Elizabeth to the sultan of Turkey in 1593, on which

> . . . two personagis which stood on to corners of the second storie, houlding tow silver trumpetes in there handes, did lifte them to theire heades, and sounded a tantarra. Then the musique went of, and the orgon played a song of 5 partes twyse over. In the tope of the orgon, being 16 foute high, did stande a holly bushe full of blacke birds and thrushis, which at the end of the musick did singe and shake theire wynges. . . .

But none of these gave any indication of what was to come. Paris was spellbound when, in 1738, the first mechanical musician burst into their ken. This was a Dresden-like flautist, the work of Jaques de Vaucanson of Grenoble. Five and a half feet high, it leaned languorously against a rock with the elegance of a classical faun. In its long hands it held a flute, down which it blew a series of airs and dances ; giving the impression, with its embroidered britches, flounced shirt, and elegant rusticity, of having just sprung from a picture by Lancret. Its pagan freedom is probably the result of Vaucanson's repressed youth, during which his only diversion was that of accompanying his mother and two other religious ladies to the local convent.

It was in the convent that his interest in mechanics began. During services he would gaze at a huge clock, trying to discover, from the parts visible to him, how it worked. Eventually he made a clock of his own from the only material available to him, which was wood. Later he constructed some priests who performed mass, and angels which flapped their wings.

The idea of a mechanical flautist came to him some years later in the Tuilleries where, entranced by the statue of a faun, he resolved to make one like it, producing real music from its instrument. He devoted to this task the pertinacity which had previously gone to discovering the mechanism of the clock. He laboured in secret ; but after three years his radiant enthusiasm attracted the notice of neighbours who began to gossip. An uncle heard of this, and would have forced him into a respectable job had he not disappeared to the country just in time. Here he worked for another three years, got into trouble with the money-lenders, and contracted a fever which drove him to his bed for sixty days. However, he continued to plan in his head, and on rising was able to begin construction at once.

As the flautist neared completion Vaucanson became more and more distracted, even ordering his ancient servant, who had followed him on all his travels, out of the house. But the old man had something of his master's secret and spent hours gazing through the keyhole. He watched as Vaucanson fixed the final cogs and set the machinery in motion. Then, as the automaton articulated its first plaintive notes, he rushed in and threw himself at the knees of his master, 'who then appeared to him more than a God.' They embraced fervently, with tears streaming down their faces. The flautist, immobile, continued its air.

It was an astonishing achievement, since for almost every note produced on the flute the strength of wind has to be varied and the position of lips and fingers altered. At first no one believed that this could be done mechanically. A concealed set of organ pipes was suspected. But, with the approval of the *Académie des Sciences*, Vaucanson published an account which silenced further criticism. The wind, it said, is supplied by bellows in the automaton's belly. These are worked by clockwork, which also turns a barrel-and-pin-mechanism operating fifteen levers, of which four work the lips so that they may be 'closed, opened, advanced, or withdrawn,' and one 'a little moveable tongue which opens and closes the windpipe.' Three more regulate the force of the wind supplied to the mouth and the rest the movements of the fingers.

Vaucanson soon produced a companion for his flautist, 'one performing on the galoubet and accompanying himself on the tambour.' This combination of pipe and drum was a common one, onomato-poeiaically known in England as 'Whittle and Dub.' There were, of course, imitations ; two flautists made for the Palace of Versailles by de France, one of which anticipated the habits of modern jazz players by 'beating time on the floor with its foot' ; a flageolet player of Pradel of Carcassone who could 'execute any piece of music for that instrument, on being allowed an hour to study it beforehand' ; another pair of flautists, made by l'Abbe Michal in 1750, who later destroyed them on being reproached with their nakedness ; and a Turk made by Gallmayr of Munich, which, 'when one demanded if he was disposed to play, replied distinctly "yes".' Later inventions of Vaucanson included a duck which quacked, ate, went in search of grain, seized it with its beak 'avec le gloutonnerie naturelle à son espèce,' and then digested it.

So far, mechanical musicians had confined themselves to woodwind,

Engraving by Vivares after Gravelot, from *An Account of an Image playing the German Flute*, by M. Vaucanson, 1742.

but in 1774 there arrived in Paris a young lady who performed on organ and clavichord. She was the work of Henri Jaquet Droz, and contemporary illustrations call her Marianne Droz. She is often illustrated with her 'brothers'—Charles Droz (*écrivain*) and Henri

'Marianne Droz.' The keyboard is in two segments
to coincide with her arms, which pivot at the elbow.

Droz (*dessinateur*). The latter, barefooted and wearing large floppy
hats, seem to be about fifteen years old ; but Marianne (now in the
Museum of History at Neuchâtel) has the beauty of a perpetual
eighteen. Beneath the fashionable flounces of her dress her breathing is
apparent and, in the words of a contemporary writer, 'the audience is
as charmed by the appearance of the *musicienne* as they are by her music.'
He continues, 'Behold her ready to play ; she leans daintily forward as
if to read the notes more easily. Then she embarks on some *pavane*
or other delicate air of former days. In astonishment we listen to her
performance, which all too soon comes to an end. The gracious artist
then resumes her upright position and, sensible of the compliments of
the audience, makes a beautiful curtsey. Her gaze, traversing the
assembly as if to assure herself of her success, forces us to demand of
her a second performance. . . . How truly beautiful she is. . . .'

Marianne Droz is worked by a barrel with pins which operates
levers going to the fingers by way of the elbows. The position of the
arms over the keys is regulated by two pivots (also at the elbow), and
other levers control the movement of eyes, head, breathing, and the
curtseying. The fame of Marianne spread over all Europe ; at the
building where she was housed 'crowds collected as if for a pilgrimage ;

the garden and highway were daily filled with carriages'; and the automaton who now rests so demurely in Neuchâtel played in the courts of Louis XV and George III.

Famous though she was, however, some automata were to be even better known. These were the work of Beethoven's friend Maelzel. Leonard Maelzel, as one is warned in many works of reference, is not to be confused with his brother; but none agrees as to which was actually which. The irregular life of Leonard necessitated occasional changes in identity; for, although a great inventor, he was an even greater cad.

A prodigy pianist at fourteen, he began his career in a characteristically grand way by creating a whole orchestra of automata, of which 'the violinists distinguished themselves particularly by the extreme agility of their fingers, the grace with which they managed their bows, the sensitivity of their interpretation and the clarity of their execution.' This was the Panharmonicon, to be enlarged, sold and recreated several times during his life. Consisting of forty-two players, it boasted flutes, clarinets, trumpets, violins and cellos, while the percussion section (according to contemporary fashion in the hands of black men) consisted of 'drums, tambours, timbals, triangles, and bells.' It played music by Haydn, Mozart (the *Magic Flute* overture), Crescentini, Spontini and Gluck; and for it Cherubini wrote a 'celebrated piece with echo effects.'

Maelzel then invented the ear-trumpet that was so useful to Beethoven. Perhaps it was the ear-trumpet which brought them together. Certainly they became friends, and they planned a visit to London with the Panharmonicon. Beethoven wrote, to Maelzel's specifications, a piece for the latter entitled *The Battle of Vittoria*, with imitations of 'bullet shots' and 'cries of the wounded.'

In view of the pernicious influence of Maelzel on Beethoven's music it is perhaps a good thing that their friendship was short-lived. To begin with, however, the association was a success. They gave two concerts in Paris, consisting of *The Battle of Vittoria*, the *Seventh Symphony*, and marches played by a mechanical trumpeter. What the symphony can have sounded like played by mechanical musicians is a matter for conjecture. The effect probably belonged to that musical limbo which also contains the *Hallelujah Chorus* arranged for two flutes. Then Beethoven discovered that Maelzel had appropriated a copy of the *Battle*, and angrily gave a third concert on his own, issuing a *Statement* to the musicians of London, advising them of Maelzel's caddish traits.

Maelzel's answer was to pack up the Panharmonicon—and the score—and leave for Munich. Here he exploited a metronome which he had stolen from Winkel of Amsterdam, with the result that most people still believe that we owe this invention to him. He also claimed to be the inventor of an automaton chess-player which he had bought in Vienna, and which distinguished itself by beating Louis XVIII.

Having exploited his mechanical *entourage* in Paris, he brought them to England, where the chess-player beat George IV; but some, including Edgar Allan Poe, doubted its complete automatism, and their doubts were justified when in 1826 the table on which the board was laid was found to conceal none other than Worouski, the celebrated chess champion.

Maelzel fled to America, where his success was even greater than in England, and he was soon a millionaire. His fame even spread to the offices of *The Times*. 'A mechanician,' reported that venerable paper in 1829, 'brother to the celebrated Moelzel of Vienna, has constructed in Boston a mechanical orchestra of 42 automata which execute several of the most difficult pieces of music in the most perfect manner; among others, the overtures to *Don Juan*, *Giovanni*, *Iphigenia*, and *La Vestale*.' It is clearly the Panharmonicon which is meant, and there is no reason for following *The Times* in being misled by Leonard's impersonation of his brother.

But even America began to take automata for granted, and Maelzel set out once more in search of fresh audiences. It was thus engaged, on a voyage to the West Indies, that he perished on the brig *Otis* in August, 1838.

Mechanical music did not die with Maelzel. In the year of his death Oeckelen of Breda, already well known as the inventor of the

Automaton clarinettist, accompanied by his inventor, Oeckelen of Breda.

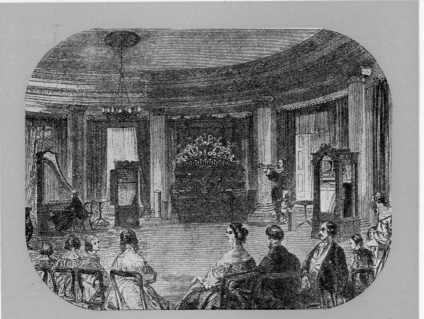

Queen Victoria listening to the Kauffmanns' automatic trumpeter, 1851

Salpinorgon (a sort of nineteenth-century cinema organ) produced a clarinettist who 'on the machinery being set in motion takes out a clarinet, wets the reed once or twice with his lips, and then performs compositions by de Beriot, Weber, Beethoven, and other composers, with the most extraordinary precision and skill, the inventor accompanying on the pianoforte.'

The inventor, in the illustration in *Musikalische Zeitung*, 1838, smiles benignly and parentlike at the virtuosity of his creation ; perhaps the creation of automata is the nearest men can get to the joys of motherhood.

A few years later the brothers Kauffmann were exhibiting a mechanical trumpeter to the Queen and Royal Family at Buckingham Palace. The trumpeter, now in the Deutsches Museum, Munich, was accompanied by four vast 'musical boxes,' the Orchestrion, Chordaulodion, Symphonion, and Harmonichord. Weber wrote 'with the help of the Kauffmanns' an '*adagio* and *rondo* for the harmonichord.' He also wrote an article on their trumpeter and was particularly impressed by a 'very beautiful double trill from f to d.'

Maskelyne and Cooke's automata at the Egyptian Hall

But the days of musical automata were numbered. The century since the Great Exhibition has produced only two worthy to be set beside the harpsichordist of Droz or the violinist of Mareppe. And these, symbolic of their times, performed on the instruments of the brass band rather than of the symphony orchestra.

They were the property of the magician Maskelyne, who exhibited them at his famous Egyptian Hall. They were the joint work of Maskelyne and a bluff Lincolnshire farmer who one day walked into his office and announced that he had invented a mechanical man capable of arithmetic, spelling, and smoking. Maskelyne immediately deserted his show and travelled with the farmer to Lincolnshire where, in an outhouse, an automaton was reclining. Maskelyne suggested a few modifications, and it materialized into the famous Psycho, after whom even racehorses and overcoats were named. Psycho was joined by Zoë, but both of these had to take second place to a pair of musicians. The first, a cornet player called Fanfare, gave his first concert in April, 1878, at which he played 'I know a bank whereon the wild thyme grows,' and joined in the duet 'Hearts and Homes' with his owner.   Later Labial, a euphonium player, made his appearance, and Maskelyne frequently played trios with his two automata, taking a third part on cornet or tenor horn. But his technique was inferior to theirs.

'Fanfare and Labial,' wrote Maskelyne's son Jasper, 'were scholarly little men with the long locks and dreamy eyes of true musicians.   One sat on a chair, the other on a music stool. They performed sweetly and accurately any popular piece of music asked for by the audience. No works were apparent, no clockwork ticking or whirring was audible, there were no electric wires or airpipe connections.   There they sat, mysterious, complacent, and earnest, and a good deal more human than some modern musicians I have met' (*White Magic*, 1936).

A. J. Phasey, solo euphonium player to Queen Victoria, was so impressed by the performance of his mechanical rival that he wrote a letter to the *Musical World* about it : 'Sir— . . . When the curtain rose I could scarcely bring myself to believe that "Labial" was not a living being, so correct was his attitude. . . . He astonished me by his truly wonderful performance of the "Death of Nelson" which was accompanied by Mr Charles Mellon. . . . Mr Maskelyne and the automaton which he has named "Fanfare" also accompanying with two cornets.' He was both delighted and depressed, 'the latter from fearing lest, at some future time, living performers in orchestras may be replaced in favour of automata.'

Phasey's prophecy has not come true. There were no successors to Labial, and, faced with the rivalry of gramophone and wireless, it is doubtful whether mechanical musicians will ever raise their clockwork heads again. But where have they gone ? The clavichordist of Droz and the trumpeter of Kauffmann are still with us, but of the rest there is little trace. The automata of Vaucanson were pawned in Nuremberg, where they remained until 1787—and then disappeared.   Another automaton, in the days of the Terror, is said to have been 'broken and despoiled, and scattered in the mud before his inventor's door.' Many perished in the fire at the *Musée Americain* in 1865, and a number may have disappeared with Maelzel on his last voyage. But even so there are many which are unaccounted for. They have vanished with the age for which they were produced ; but I cannot resist the belief that, to this day, in some deserted museum or antique shop, an assembly of moth-eaten automata bow elegantly to non-existent audiences or trill through imaginary encores.

THE SWAN SONG OF STEAM

by L. T. C. ROLT

HE PLANS announced this year for the future of British Railways forecast the ultimate disappearance of the steam engine. Already steam recedes into the mists of history. Where are the steam engines of yesteryear? Where, indeed? The old power that drove the wheels of industrial revolution has stolen away to the scrap-yard, has gone back to the molten womb of the furnace that bore it. Its passing is mourned only by a devoted few, for in the deafening mechanical bedlam of this atomic age we have no ears for the swan song of steam.

The more modern the motive power the more brutal is its assault upon our nerves and ear drums. Certainly, compared with its successors, steam is a silent power. After the crude explosions of the internal combustion engine or the demonic howl of the 'jet' the voice of the old reciprocating steam engine is as soothing as a lullaby. Its exhaust noise is never more than an impatient snort when suddenly roused, and is usually a mere sigh of escaping steam. And, mechanically, how smooth is the majestic sweep of the long connecting rod, how beautifully ordered the dance of the eccentrics and the silent sword-play of the shining valve-rods ! The engineer understands this magic of the steam engine, but he cannot put it into words. Of the poets, only Kipling could express it truly. Listen to McAndrew, his old Scots engineer :

> Lord, send a man like Robbie Burns to sing the Song o' Steam !
> To match wi' Scotia's noblest speech yon orchestra sublime
> Whaurto—uplifted like the Just—the tail rods mark the time.
> The crank-throws give the double-bass, the feed-pump sobs and heaves,
> An' now the main eccentrics start their quarrel on the sheaves :
> Her time, her own appointed time, the rocking link-head bides,
> Till—hear that note ?—the rod's return whings glimmerin' through the
> guides.

McAndrew's hymn of praise celebrates the fascination of a power which, like the wind that filled the sails of a full-rigged ship or the water under the mill wheel, a future generation will never know. When it was written in 1893 the steam engine was at the zenith of its power and pride. The internal combustion engine was no more than a stuttering mechanical joke in questionable engineering taste. Even the steam turbine had not begun to oust piston and crank from the sea, for it was not until 1895 that Sir Charles Parsons launched his revolutionary *Turbinia*. How swiftly has that pride fallen ! We have lived to see steam banished from road and river, field and fairground, even as it will soon lose its dominion over the rail and the sea.

While our modern machines may convey the impression of power to the ear, visually man has created no embodiment of power more impressive than that oldest of steam engines, the stationary beam-engine. To watch one of these mighty machines at work, to see the huge beam rocking to and fro, high overhead in the shadowy engine-house, and the gleaming piston-rods sweeping down with a heavy sigh into a cylinder six feet or more in diameter, is to appreciate why they were once regarded with such awe. Draining the mine, blowing the furnace, turning the loom, the beam-engine was the mechanical Prometheus of the eighteenth century. The Devonian Thomas

Newcomen invented it, as a non-rotative pump, as early as 1712, and James Watt later perfected it. Where they have not been entirely demolished, most of the tall engine-houses in which the products of Boulton & Watt's famous Soho Foundry once laboured now stand empty and ruinous. Yet a few, very few, such as the Crofton canal pumping station on the fringe of Savernake Forest, are still tenanted by working engines, and have thus become places of devout pilgrimage for steam enthusiasts. The Newcomen Society, whose headquarters are at the Science Museum in London, and its offshoot, the Cornish Engine Preservation Society, have between them done much to ensure the permanent preservation in working order of a few choice examples.

These massive beam-engines were not only extraordinarily long-lived but, with detail improvements, they continued to be built over a very long period of years. The tradition established by Boulton & Watt in the eighteenth century was carried forward in the nineteenth by other engineers, notably by that great Cornish firm, Harveys of Hayle. In 1843 Harveys built a pumping engine for draining Haarlem Lake which had a cylinder 12 feet in diameter and 12 feet in length. Twenty-five tons of metal were melted in three furnaces to cast this immense cylinder, which Harveys proudly claimed to be the largest ever cast for any purpose. Erected and set to work in Holland in 1849, this steam titan proceeded to labour without interruption until 1933 —eighty-four years ! Many years later, when the Great Western Railway's Severn Tunnel works appeared to be doomed owing to the inrush of what was called the 'Great Spring,' it was Harveys of Hayle who came to the rescue. Between 1883 and 1886 the firm supplied six 10 foot stroke 'Cornish' beam-engines whose combined efforts drained the drowned workings and have kept the Great Spring in check to this day. These were among the last big beam-engines to be built in England.

As a result of the rapid technical advances made during the railway building age, steam engines of much lighter, simpler and handier form were evolved and applied to a vast range of new duties, both stationary and mobile. The main reason for this was the improvement in boiler-making technique which made the use of high-pressure steam a practical proposition. The early beam-engines used steam at little above atmospheric pressure, and their monumental scale became no longer necessary when a steam pressure of 100 pounds per square inch became commonplace. For all but the heaviest duties the ponderous beam-engine was superseded by a machine incomparably lighter and of a classical simplicity and elegance. Thus, to take but one example, the machinery of that almost extinct craft, the Thames steam launch, with its mahogany cabinwork and gleaming brass funnel, represents, by contrast with the engines of the first iron steamships, the ultimate refinement of the reciprocating steam engine in this sphere.

Because of their sheer size the early beam-engines were the product of comparatively few specialist manufacturers, and, because of their

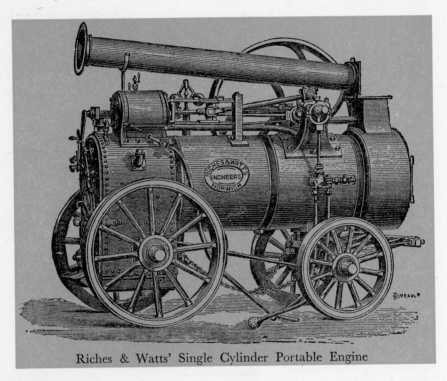

Riches & Watts' Single Cylinder Portable Engine

complexity, the same is true of our internal combustion and 'jet' engines today. But in that Golden Age of steam, the second half of the nineteenth century, it was quite otherwise. Manufacture of the smaller and simpler engines of this period did not call for any great outlay in capital equipment and could be undertaken by the average country foundry. As a result it could be said with some truth that throughout this brief heyday steam-engine building became a new rural craft. There was scarcely a small seaport on our coast that could not boast a builder of marine steam engines, scarcely a market

[267]

town where steam traction or the simpler horse-drawn 'portable' engines were not built for the local farmers.

In any market town where there is an old-established agricultural engineering business the odds are that this firm, which now distributes mass-produced tractors and combine harvesters, once built steam engines. In Norfolk alone, a purely agricultural county, a local expert, Mr Ronald Clark, has traced no less than thirty-one steam-engine builders. Nor were these confined to the larger towns. North Walsham, Acle, Diss, Scole, Marsham and Great Ryburgh all had their steam engineers. And what beautiful, and occasionally weird and wonderful, machines these countrymen built !

The Norfolk list includes two firms whose very names are sufficient to conjure up for the middle-aged all the magic of the fairgrounds of our youth—Savages of King's Lynn, and Burrells of Thetford, household words, both, to showmen when steam reigned supreme. What if our children do derive as much pleasure from the modern fair with its roaring, stinking diesel engines and its doleful canned music blaring forth from worn-out gramophone records ? They can never know the fascination and romance that was lost when these modern inventions banished steam and the steam-driven organ from the market place.

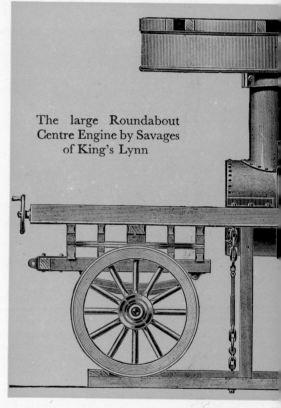

The large Roundabout Centre Engine by Savages of King's Lynn

One of the greatest thrills of the fair for myself as a small boy was to steal away from the noise and the bright lights to that retired corner where two, or perhaps even three, great Burrell showmen's engines, resplendent in scarlet paint and glittering brass-work, stood side by side in the shadows, tall extension chimneys reaching to the October starlight and carrying the flying lamp-lit steam high above the house-tops. How effortlessly they spun the humming dynamos hour after hour as they rocked gently to and fro on their enormous rubber-shod wheels and exuded that inimitable smell of hot cylinder oil which was incense to a steam-struck boy.

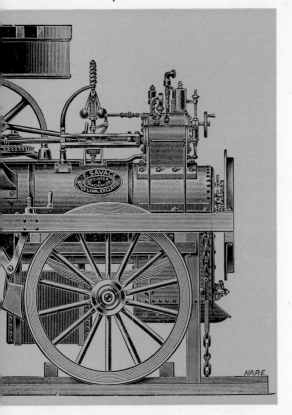

Yet even these Bur-rells, with their electric generators, represented the first step towards the modern fairground. Go back a few more years and we find that the roundabouts, the 'gallopers,' are directly steam-driven. It was in the manufacture of these that Savages of King's Lynn excelled. The heart of the steam galloper was the Centre Engine, a small port-able steam engine and boiler mounted in a four-wheeled wagon frame for transport. Around this engine the glittering outfit was quickly built. Driven by gearing from the engine, a large horizontal wheel whose bearing was the base of the chimney formed the hub of the revolving platform on which the horses pranced, while the long chimney itself became the centre pole of the canopy. In addition, all the best Centre Engines had two essential accessories. One was a special steam siren whose excited whoops were irresistible. More eloquent and persuasive than any showman's patter, and more penetrating than any public address amplifier, it was guaranteed to bring townsfolk and villagers flocking from near and far.

[269]

The first engine made to drive a Roundabout, by S. G. Soame of Marsham

To dark, owl-haunted country lanes far from the garish
lights that siren call would
carry, on still autumn nights :
'Whoooo...oop! The fair's
in town, hurry, hurry !'

The second accessory,
often mounted on the Centre
Engine's smoke-box, was the
Organ Engine, an exquisite
miniature, also built by
Savages, which drove the
organ by a long, slender
belt. These organs, now,
alas, extremely rare, were
the most supreme and superb
examples of fairground rococo, and as important a part of
the steam roundabout as the horses themselves. It is no wonder
that the gallopers lost popularity to dodgems and other more modern
attractions so soon as they lost their organs. The little steam engine so
sweetly spinning, the miniature plaster pantomime figures nodding,
striking their bells, and clashing their cymbals, the punched sheets of
music so miraculously and neatly folding themselves as the organ
disgorged them—has the ingenuity of man ever conceived anything so
finely calculated to captivate and entrance the eye of a child ? And the
sound of it ! That pulse-quickening tweedle-dee from the massed pipes
sounding crescendo-diminuendo each time we circled round clinging
with sweaty palms to the 'barley sugar' brass rail which speared our steed.

In fact, although the name of Savage became so famous on the fairground, the firm were highly successful exploiters rather than pioneers
in this fascinating by-way of steam engineering. The first man to
apply steam power to a roundabout and the first to produce a steam
Organ Engine was Sidney George Soame, of Marsham. In the early
'seventies, Soame built a charming little steam portable engine to
drive a children's roundabout. On its first public appearance at a fair
at Aylsham it was seen by Frederick Savage who realized its commercial
possibilities and possessed resources which Soame lacked.

Fair engines might be termed the exotics of the steam world, and
even such firms as Burrell and Savage who excelled in them did not

rely exclusively upon them for their bread and butter. In company with a host of other country engineering firms, few of whose names are remembered today, they catered primarily for the agricultural industry. The thousands of steam engines which were supplied to farmers and agricultural contractors before the advent of the tractor ranged from the humble horse-drawn 'Portable' to the big cable ploughing engine. Although they lacked the glamorous frills of the fair engine, in their prime even these workaday machines were eye-catchers, with their lustrous and seemingly indestructible paintwork elaborately lined out and their polished brass boiler-lagging bands. In order to win over a generation of farmers who took a pride in beautifully turned out wagons and teams the steam engine had to be finely finished and 'brassed up.'

Basically, the design of the modest 'Portable' hardly changed from the time of its introduction in the 1850s until the small petrol or diesel engine drove it into limbo. Some of the first self-propelled engines were little more than Portables fitted with a long chain-drive connecting the crankshaft to the rear wheels. Indeed, one early type of farmer's self-propelled engine was still 'horse steered,' the theory being that horses would be less likely to bolt at sight of the fearsome machine if they saw one of their brothers plodding between shafts in front.

The second Savory Ploughing Engine as developed by Richard Garrett

This idea was short-lived. Perhaps there was a shortage of suitably steam-minded horses to do the steering. Later, the orthodox form of the traction engine was evolved when gears took the place of driving chains and, as a result, the engine was mounted the other way round on the top of the boiler. All these engines, both Portable and self-propelled, conformed very closely to a common pattern. It was in the design of special engines for cultivating and ploughing that the agricultural engineers achieved the most extraordinary flights of inventive fancy. At a remarkably early date weird forms of driving wheel were evolved which anticipated the modern 'caterpillar' track ; fearsome-looking 'steam diggers' appeared with rows of revolving tines driven by an astonishing gallimaufry of exposed shafts and cog wheels.

These cumbersome and complicated monsters, like the dinosaur, had little survival value and soon became extinct. It was realized that the heavy steam engine was better off the arable field. Could not the engine stand on the headland and haul a plough or a cultivator across the field by means of a steel cable ? The engineer's answer was the cable ploughing-engine. There were many strange variants of the cable engine at first, notably a type designed by Savory, of Gloucester, which had a large cable-drum encircling the boiler barrel. But the

The early Savage Geared Traction

definitive type, whose most successful and prolific maker was John Fowler, of Leeds, had the drum mounted horizontally beneath the boiler. Given the right conditions, a pair of these great Fowler ploughing-engines hauling a five- or six-furrow 'balanced plough' back and forth across the stubble made a remarkably efficient combination. But the tractor has ousted them. Surviving sets of steam ploughing tackle could probably be counted on the fingers today. Some lie rusting among the nettles at the back of farm or contractors' yards while many more have fallen a prey to the scrap-metal merchant's torch.

The same is true of the smaller agricultural engines, but they have earned a permanent place in the affection of every countryman. Our children will know only the tractor and the combine harvester but, just as an older generation could recall with nostalgia the thwack of the flail on the threshing floor, so we shall remember always that plume of steam over the stackyard on misty autumn mornings and the drone of the threshing drum rising and falling as the sheaves were fed in.

I have often wondered why so many of these old farm engines survived for so long and faded away so unobtrusively instead of coming to a violently explosive end. For I can testify from personal experience that boiler inspectors could be very accommodating after they had been sufficiently primed with cider or home-made wine. The farmer's cellar, or, failing that, a convivial session in the village pub, must have reprieved many an ageing boiler. As for the stalwart countrymen who drove these old engines, the possibility of sudden dissolution certainly never worried them. Perhaps it just never occurred to them. I once knew an ancient man, driver of a Fowler steam ploughing-engine which was nearly as old as himself, who habitually screwed down the safety valve if he wanted more power. While the more imaginative and pessimistic onlookers retreated to a safe distance he would wait patiently on his footplate, placidly puffing at his pipe, until pressure had built up sufficiently for the engine to pull the load. 'He'll do that once too often,' we thought ; yet we were wrong, for both he and his engine came to a peaceful end.

On the road, steam has been no less effectually routed. What has become of the steam wagons—the Fodens, Sentinels, Claytons, Yorkshires and Robeys—that once we knew ? Their very names, so familiar once, will soon be forgotten. When he must perforce follow behind one as it snorted up a steep hill and a fine rain of cinders pattered down on the roof of his car, the motorist of yesterday felt little affection for the steam wagon. Yet when today, enveloped in a cloud of acrid black smoke, we are forced to crawl in the wake of the all-conquering diesel lorry, we may reflect that we are really no better off for the passing of steam. At least the steamer had a less offensive smell. And is it imagination, or did the steam wagon breed a happier, more rubicund and more philosophical school of drivers? Certainly you could tell a steam man from the driver of a petrol lorry as easily as you could distinguish a cabby from a taxi driver.

One exemplar of steam on the road is still with us in fair strength—the steam-roller. Just as the name of Burrell of Thetford spelt showman's engines so that of Aveling & Porter, of Rochester, meant road rollers, although many other firms built them. So prolific was the output of Avelings that their trade mark, the rearing horse of Kent proudly displayed in polished brass, came to be looked upon by many people as a mystic traditional device peculiar to all steam-rollers. But, like the traction engine and the steam wagon before it, the steam-roller is now unobtrusively fading away. No statistics record changes such as this, but every year a few more steamers are replaced by diesel rollers, and it seems very probable that within the next decade we shall suddenly realize the fact that the steamer has become extinct. Lumbering, clanking and snorting, the old steam-roller was always regarded as rather a joke, an elephantine clown of a machine. Yet we have these uncouth monsters to thank for thousands of miles of smooth roads, and before they pass into oblivion we should appreciate the immensity of the task they have accomplished.

It is hardly practicable for your steam enthusiast to acquire a full-scale railway engine, and even if he did he would have to obtain 'running powers' from the British Transport Commission over some abandoned branch line before he could exercise it. But the road locomotive is a machine capable of inspiring a similar affection and its operation does not involve the same difficulty. There are problems, of course, which scarcely need stressing. For example, a Tasker 'Little Giant' would be a most desirable collector's item, but even this, one of the smallest road-engines ever built commercially, would carry away the roof of the average garage with its chimney. As a hobby, it must be admitted that the collection of traction engines is scarcely practicable for the townsman. Even if he could solve the accommodation difficulty, relations with his next-door neighbours and the local authorities might well become more than a little strained. Nevertheless, although the maintenance and running of a traction engine presents almost as many problems as keeping an elephant, a number of these fine old machines *are* being preserved in working order as the growing popularity of traction-engine 'meets' both in the north and south of England testifies. But because steam traction-engines were primarily country bred so, naturally, except for a few who enjoy special facilities, it is the tradition-loving countryman who has been able to find house room for the veterans of this once great army.

Still on Tour

Although the use of the horse on the farm is so rapidly dying out, we still have classes for shire horses at our leading agricultural shows. In view of the growing interest in these survivors of the great age of steam, is it too much to hope that we may soon see a parade of traction engines, restored to their former glory, snorting proudly round the show ring ? Like the shire horse, they gave yeoman service in days gone by, and to accord them this recognition would be an appropriate and graceful tribute to the enduring workmanship of that bygone generation of country engineers who built them.

The Editor is indebted to Mr Ronald H. Clark, author of several books on the steam engine builders of East Anglia, for the provision of illustrations to this article.

[275]

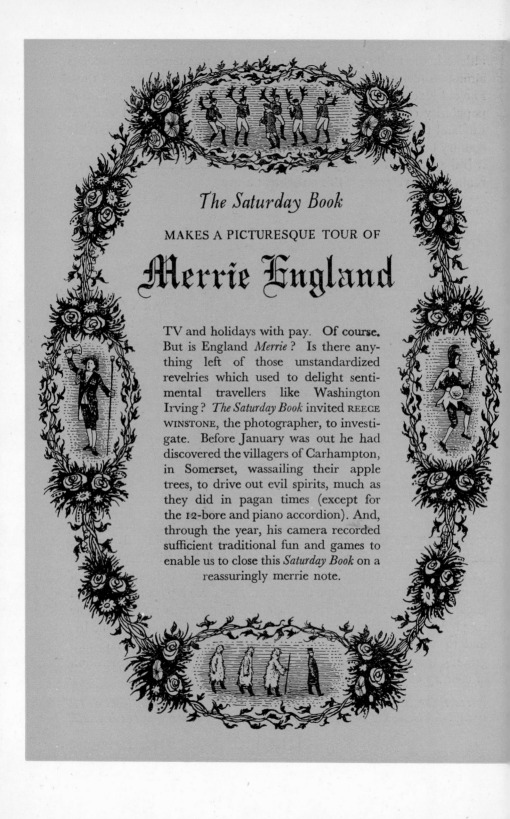

The Saturday Book

MAKES A PICTURESQUE TOUR OF

Merrie England

TV and holidays with pay. Of course.
But is England *Merrie*? Is there anything left of those unstandardized
revelries which used to delight senti-
mental travellers like Washington
Irving? *The Saturday Book* invited REECE
WINSTONE, the photographer, to investi-
gate. Before January was out he had
discovered the villagers of Carhampton,
in Somerset, wassailing their apple
trees, to drive out evil spirits, much as
they did in pagan times (except for
the 12-bore and piano accordion). And,
through the year, his camera recorded
sufficient traditional fun and games to
enable us to close this *Saturday Book* on a
reassuringly merrie note.

Shrove Tuesday—or Saturnalia ? Whilst the swans prepare to count their cygnets the curious ceremony of Egg Shackling is being enacted in the Somerset villages of Stoke St Gregory and Shepton Beauchamp. Each child brings an egg to school, marked with his or her name. In a sieve (padded, we notice, with 'comics') the eggs are gently shaken ('shackled') until, one by one, they crack and are removed, to make pancakes. The owner of the egg with the toughest shell gets a prize, provided annually by an ancient legacy.

Food is a prime ingredient of Merriement. The choir boys of St Michael's Church, Bristol, still enjoy the 'twopenny starvers' they traditionally receive on Easter Tuesday.

Meanwhile, each year on Lady Day, Sir Anthony Tichborne distributes flour to his tenants on the steps of Tichborne House, near Winchester. The Tichborne 'Dole' or 'Crawl' originated in the twelfth century when Sir Roger promised Lady Mabella, on her death-bed, that he would annually give bread to all the poor living on the ground round which she could walk with a lighted torch in her hand. She could only crawl, but she encircled 23 acres before she died, laying a curse on her family if the gift be forgotten.

Kingsteignton, in South Devon, is one of the villages where May Day still means dancing round the Maypole and the election of a May Queen. On the same day the Hobby Horse parades the streets of Minehead wearing a fearsome cardboard mask. To those who give him money the Hobby Horse gravely bows : others are lashed by his tail. His ancestry goes back beyond the Morris Dance, and may commemorate a time when armed men rode on ponies to protect the Somerset and Cornish coasts from marauders.

May traditionally comes in with song at the Universities, notably at Magdalen College, Oxford. We find much the same ceremony being enacted on the tower of St Stephens Church, Bristol. As the month comes to an end Cambridge celebrates the 'Mays' with the annual sport of 'bumping,' when fifteen or so crews struggle for leadership on the river Cam, to the vocal encouragement of innumerable cyclists.

June rhymes with Moon. Young lovers dream of the day when the bench in the park is replaced by a three-piece suite and a 'telly' of one's own. But the proud owner of Little Dunster Castle, Somerset, is content to share it with his dog, and Mr Uriah Lovell, chair-maker, cheerfully lives alone in the woods at Porthmerion, N. Wales.

The Merriest note in Merrie England—certainly the one that echoes farthest—is that of the famous Furry, or Floral Dance, which takes place at Helston, in Cornwall, on May 8, the Feast of the Apparition of St. Michael, patron saint of the borough. The name, Furry, derives from the word *fer*, a fair, which in turn comes from the Latin, *feria*, meaning a holy day. The dancers in morning dress and floral frocks dance through the streets, passing through houses on their merry way. There is a traditional dance tune, but the popular ballad by Katie Moss is of twentieth-century origin—like the unwitting humour of the Bristol street signs on the left.

In Hungerford, Berkshire, which is governed by an elected Constable, Portreeve and Bailiff, there are ceremonies at Hocktide—the Tuesday after Easter week —which go back to the days of John of Gaunt. Two elected Tutti-men, armed with beflowered and beribboned tutti-poles, and each holding an orange, parade the town demanding a coin from every man and a kiss from every woman (for which an orange is given in exchange). They are accompanied by an Orange Man (with sack), whose hat is decorated with cock's feathers. Visitors and strangers have to undergo the strenuous ceremony of 'Shoeing the Colt.' *Picture Post Library*

At daybreak on Oak Apple Day oak branches are brought from Grovely Wood to decorate the houses. At noon the Oak Apple Club begin their festivities with a procession through the village, past the thirteenth-century church and the bough-decked cottages. First comes a banner bearing the ancient Grovely declaration, then four women bearing bundles of kindlings on their heads, then a company of men bearing huge boughs on their shoulders, and finally an assembly of villagers in fancy dress. The celebration continues on the village fairground through the afternoon.

On Oak Apple Day, May 29—the birthday of King Charles II—the villagers of Wishford, near Salisbury, claim their ancient right to gather kindling in Grovely wood and to cut, once each year, the largest branches of green wood they can carry by hand. It is said that one of the Earls of Pembroke tried to remove this privilege, but a woman, Grace Reed, rallied the villagers, and proved that the right belonged to the people.

Every Whit Monday in Bampton, Oxfordshire, an 80-year old fiddler, 'Jingle' Wells, leads a troupe of Morris Dancers, from early morning until late at night, through the village streets, into the Doctor's garden (where you see them here), across the Squire's lawn, and to the annual fête. Mr Wells has done this for sixty years, and his family before him for two hundred years. Behind him, on the ground, is his traditional bowler hat, with a nosegay of flowers. The dancers bear brooms as they dance to a mediaeval routine, encouraged by a clown with a bladder on a stick.

Whit Monday has been celebrated for 400 years on Coopers Hill, Witcombe, in Gloucestershire, by cheese-rolling. At six in the evening, when Tom Windo, wearing smock and top hat, gives the signal, the cheese—called 'the Round Doughnut'—is rolled down the hill, chased by the village boys. The winner is entitled to keep it. Six races are held, one for girls, and spectators come from miles around.

The painted horses of the fairground roundabout are becoming so 'period' as to be the subject of treatises on folk art. Live horses, however, still play starring parts in the ceremony of Common-Riding at Hawick, Roxburghshire, which takes place annually in the second week of June. A standard bearer, or Cornet, whose functions originated in the sixteenth century, is elected by the Town Council and 'rides the marches,' bearing the colour 'bussed' with ribbon. Festivities continue over three days, and include a ceremonial cutting of a sod, a distribution of oak leaves, the singing of the Common-Riding Song, horse-racing, and a ball at which past and present standard bearers dance the Cornet's Reel. *Picture Post*

AUGUST. The sun beats down on basking bikinis and countless outspread copies of the *Daily Mirror* which rise and fall to the steady breathing of men at ease. It is all *calme, luxe et volupté*—except at the noisome meeting-place where the Town Criers of England are holding their annual festival. Mr. C. Bethell, the Town Crier of Corsham, carries a staff and wears a three-cornered hat. Like some fifteen or twenty other Criers who have come to honour their calling, he will walk in procession to a field where he will render the set piece, a proclamation which abounds in difficult phrases and tricky syntax. If he is adjudged the winner he will take home a cash prize and will have the honour of entertaining next year's competitors on his own home pitch. Oyez! Oyez!

But why are the Town Criers always male? The lady in the Fish Market clearly has an equal command of gesture, delivery, and language. Oyez? Not b . . . likely!

'How happy could I be with either !' The two-rod man beside the River Avon would seem to have raised placidity to a fine art, though the donkeys at Weston-super-Mare run him (or walk him) close, having secured for themselves a Donkey's Charter, laying down maximum hours of work, an hour for lunch, and a day off on Sunday. Standing and staring—even at trained mice—is, of course, a hallowed relaxation ; but how much better to *sit* and stare—at the deck chess on Bournemouth Pier. Who, in so idyllic a State of Welfare, would dream of contravening *any* of the edicts reproduced below.

PORT ISAAC HARBOUR BOARD
<u>PLEASE DO NOT</u>
TOUCH THE SHELL FISH IN THE
STORE POTS   OR:-
SIT ON THE SIDES OF THE
SMALL BOATS

Notice

It is forbidden to collect peacock feathers. These may be obtained at the café.

DORSET
ANY PERSON WILFULLY INJURING
ANY PART OF THIS COUNTY BRIDGE
WILL BE GUILTY OF FELONY AND
UPON CONVICTION LIABLE TO BE
TRANSPORTED FOR LIFE
BY THE COURT
7&8 GEO 4 C30 S13   T FOOKS

TRESPASSERS WILL BE PROSECUTED

At Abbots Bromley, Staffordshire, on the first Monday after September 4 each year, twelve dancers in Tudor clothes gather at 8 a.m. on the village green. Six of them bear huge reindeer antlers, weighing up to 25 lb. There is a Jester, an archer representing Robin Hood, a lad riding a Hobby Horse, a man dressed as Maid Marian, and musicians playing a melodeon and a triangle. Together they dance round the twenty miles of the parish bounds, performing set 'figures' at Blithfield Hall and other stopping places. The Horn Dance, in which the snapping jaws of the Hobby Horse keep time to the music, symbolizes the rites of the chase and establishes the villagers' privilege of hunting in Needwood Forest, which was once the hunting ground of John of Gaunt.

Not *quite* so venerable as the Abbots Bromley Hobby Horse is this 1912 Renault, which belongs to Mr Dick Wilderspin, of Swavesey, Cambridgeshire. Despite his name we doubt if Mr Wilderspin need bother to heed Messrs Gliksten's adjuration.

The nights draw in. Beside his artlessly contrived but uncommonly cheerful hearth the Night Watchman settles down to his long vigil. Thomas Wright of Derby, one feels, would have loved to paint this scene—corrugated iron and all.

Meanwhile, with his buttonhole of crackers, Guy Fawkes waits to have his seat warmed on November 5. If he has the honour of taking part in the festivities at Lewes, in Sussex, he can be assured of a bonfire second to none, an audience of tens of thousands, and a veritable *girandole* of a funeral.

We return to food and drink. In Bristol, on December 21, a 'mighty apple pie' is prepared for the old people of Dr Thomas White's Almshouses, whose Governors will entertain the Lord Mayor to dinner. The pie will contain 99 apples and one quince, and must be cooked in a pewter dish.

Whilst the wine tasters display their expertise in the cellars of a famous firm of Bristol shippers ('Your nose will tell you almost as much as your palate') the local character whose bowler hat has leather side-straps trundles the casks across the cobblestones. The Festive Season is upon us, and the wines so delicately described as Bristol Milk and Bristol Cream will contribute to the Festivities.

Christmas has come, the turkey has been carved and *The Saturday Book* unwrapped. Now it is Boxing Day, and in the little village square at Marshfield in Gloucestershire the Mummers enact their 800-years-old play, whose characters include Old Father Christmas, Beelzebub, and the Doctor who heals the 'wounded' man with magic medicine. Alka Seltzer, perhaps? Or merely the traditional *Sod. Bicarb?*